USBORNE
ASTRONOMY
FOR BEGINNERS

Sarah Hull & Tom Mumbray

Illustrated by
Beatrix Hatcher

Designed by
Jamie Ball

Astronomy expert:
Dr. Sheila Kanani MBE

CONTENTS

INTRODUCTION 4
All about what astronomy actually is, and the role it has played in people's lives throughout history – from navigating the seas, to worshipping gods in the skies.

CHAPTER 1: WHERE ARE WE? 12
Earth's place in the universe is in the solar system, orbiting the Sun, along with seven other planets, countless space rocks and lumps of ice, and a whole load of junk.

CHAPTER 2: ALL WE CAN SEE 30
Astronomers have found out a LOT about the universe by looking through huge telescopes on Earth – and by sending probes and telescopes out into space.

CHAPTER 3: MORE THAN MEETS THE EYE 42
Stars and planets give off radiation. By studying it, astronomers can find out all sorts of things – from the temperature of a star and the chemicals it contains, to the shape of a planet's surface.

CHAPTER 4: EXPLAINING IT ALL 56
To explain how the universe works, astronomers come up with theories. These are then backed up by evidence from telescopes, lab experiments, or complicated models run on supercomputers.

CHAPTER 5: THE UNIVERSE 66
The universe expanded from a tiny dot, in a mind-blowing event called the Big Bang. But what shape is the universe? How might it end? And could there actually be more than one?

CHAPTER 6: GRAVITY 84
Gravity holds the universe together, interacting with space and time. Black holes are the regions where gravity is strongest. What would happen if you fell into one?

CHAPTER 7: IS ANYBODY OUT THERE? 100
Searching for aliens starts with a search for water, because all life we know depends on it. At the same time, people listen out for alien signals, as well as planning their own adventures in space.

CHAPTER 8: ASTRONOMY AND YOU 112
Get stuck into astronomy from your own home, or choose your ideal astronomy career. Also, find out about the everyday technology given to us by astronomy.

USBORNE QUICKLINKS

For links to websites where you can see amazing images taken by space telescopes, find out what astronomers do, and explore topics from this book with videos and activities, go to **usborne.com/Quicklinks** and enter this book's title.

Usborne Publishing is not responsible for the content of external websites. Children should be supervised online. Please follow the online safety guidelines at **usborne.com/Quicklinks**

WHAT *IS* ASTRONOMY?

Astronomy is a science. It's all about trying to understand the mysterious things that exist beyond the atmosphere surrounding Earth. It's an astronomer's job to ask questions about these things, and to search for answers.

Where do stars come from?

STARS

How many are there?

Are all planets round?

PLANETS

What happens when a star dies?

Are there any planets similar to Earth?

Could we live on other planets?

What are space rocks made of?

SPACE ROCKS
Asteroids, comets and meteoroids

Where did they all come from?

Do space rocks ever land on Earth?

LOOKING UP

People have studied the Sun, Moon and stars, and the patterns they follow, for thousands of years. Using these patterns they have been able to track time and find their way across land and sea.

Sunrise marks the start of a new day.

In prehistoric times, people built stone calendars, to follow the movements of the Sun and stars relative to Earth.

HEAVENS ABOVE

To many ancient peoples, the Sun, Moon and stars were gods. These beliefs shaped the way people thought about what was happening in the sky above them.

Can you imagine how frightening it would be if, without warning, the Sun suddenly turned dark in the middle of the day?

That's exactly what happens during a solar eclipse. The Moon passes in front of the Sun, blocking its light for a few minutes.

Today, scientists can predict exactly when and where an eclipse will be visible on Earth – even thousands of years into the future.

But thousands of years ago, eclipses took people by surprise. They came up with stories to explain what was happening...

Long, long ago in South America

We must make offerings to the Sun god. He is angry!

Meanwhile, in ancient China

A dragon is eating the Sun! Make as much noise as possible to scare it away.

BANG BANG BANG

In ancient Mesopotamia (modern-day Iraq), people believed their gods gave them clues about the future through the movements of stars, planets and the Moon. Scholars used mathematics to predict these movements, so they could stop any terrible events coming their way.

Using mathematics to study the movements of the stars was the beginning of the science of astronomy.

FINDING OUR PLACE

Astronomy is all about space, but it's important for understanding Earth, too. What we know about our place in the universe today is the result of thousands of years of ideas and research.

Many people in early civilizations believed Earth was a flat disk covered by a large dome, which was decorated with the stars.

We live in the middle of EVERYTHING!

Then, just under 2,000 years ago, ancient Greek scholar Ptolemy described a different view of the universe. It looked something like this.

Earth was a ball-like sphere, motionless in the middle of the universe.

The planets were attached to spheres which **orbited** – or moved around – the Earth.

The outer sphere holds the stars. Watch them sail past!

Ptolemy

The idea that Earth was at the middle of the universe held for over a thousand years, until...

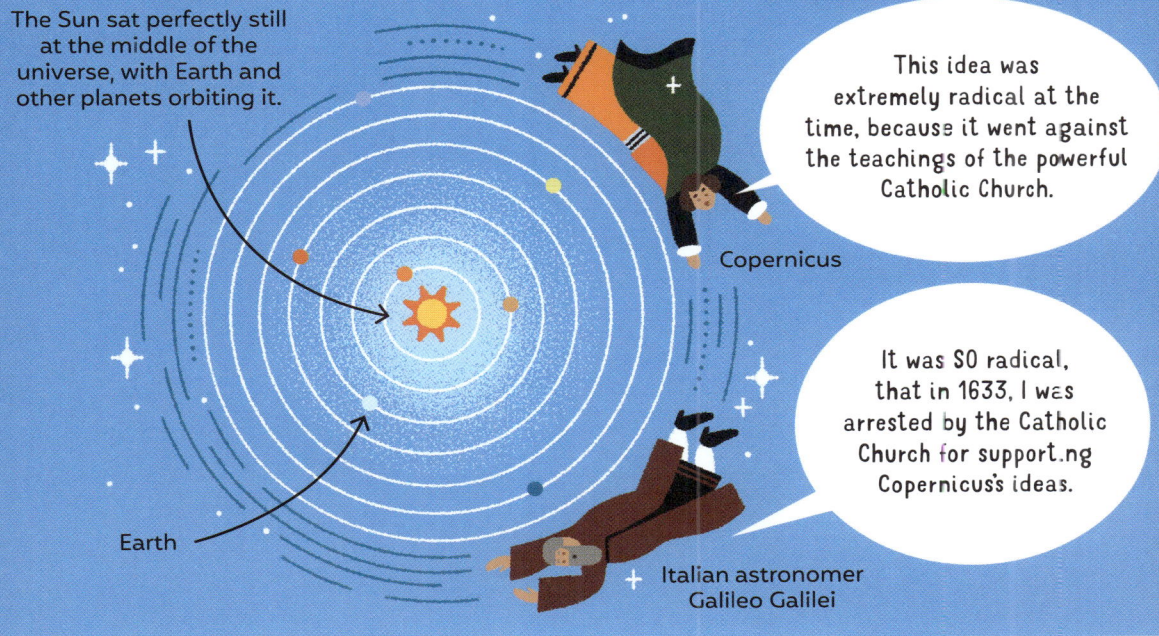

WHERE ARE WE?

The little part of space we call home is known as the solar system. It's a whirling collection of planets and space rocks – all held together by the Sun.

It's the bit of the universe we know best – on a clear night, you might even spot some nearby planets. Scientists have learned more about it by sending spacecraft and astronauts out to explore.

But in doing so, we're also changing the solar system, adding thousands of human-made objects to the mix.

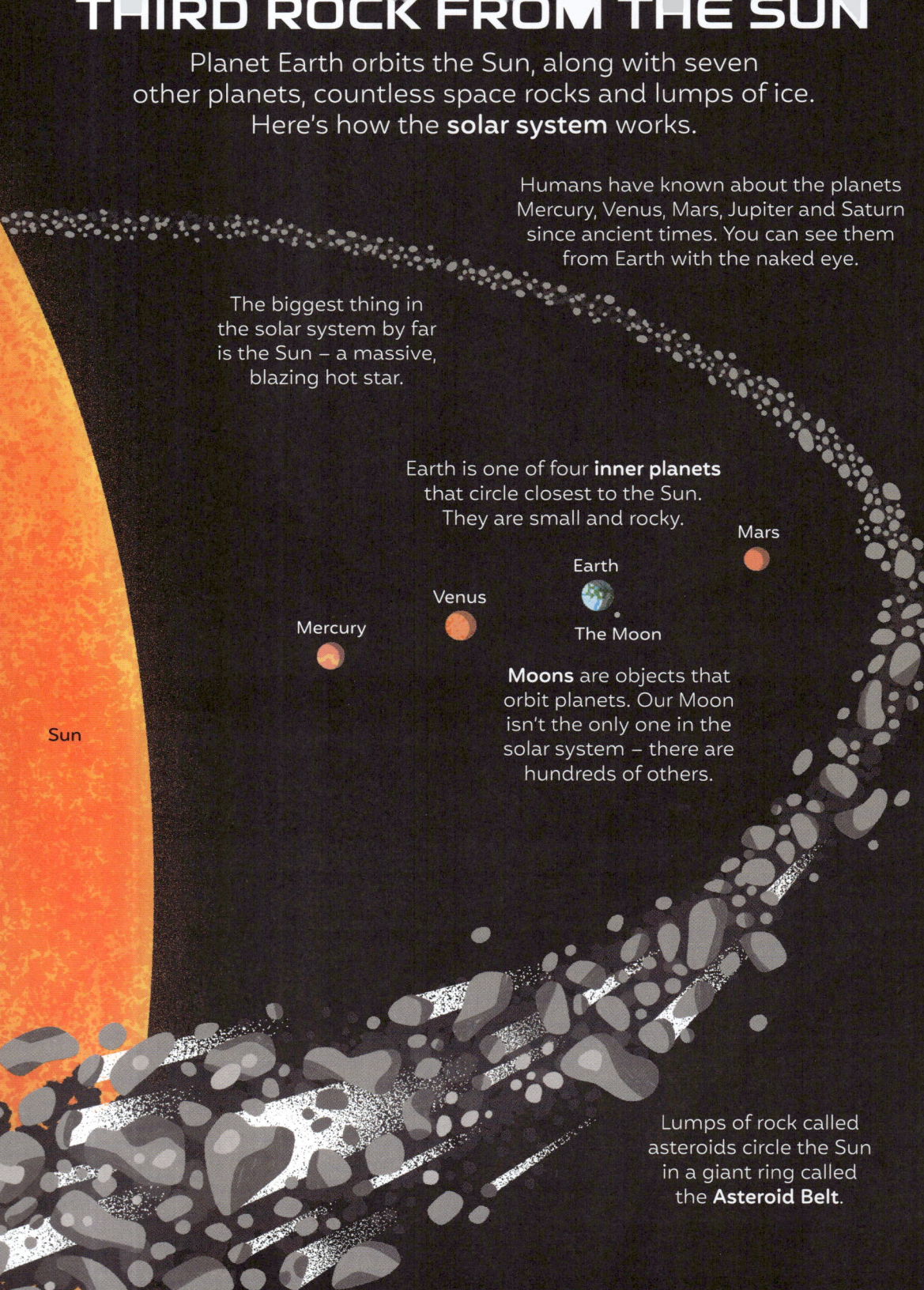

The four **outer planets** are giant balls of gas.

At last count, Jupiter had 95 moons. Its largest – Ganymede – is bigger than Mercury.

Billions of small chunks of ice and rock orbit Saturn in huge, flat rings.

Uranus was discovered in 1781, and Neptune in 1830, thanks to the invention of telescopes.

Beyond Neptune lies the **Kuiper Belt** – a ring of icy and rocky objects, including lumps of frozen water, methane and other chemicals.

This rocky object is Pluto. It's almost large enough to be a planet.

Wow, so that's the solar system!

Yeah... well, it doesn't actually look ANYTHING like this. The Sun is even bigger and everything is much, MUCH further apart.

If the Sun were the size of a basketball, the Earth would be a sesame seed at the opposite end of the basketball court.

SHOWING THE SOLAR SYSTEM

The vast distances between the planets and their huge size differences make it impossible to show the solar system accurately on a page.

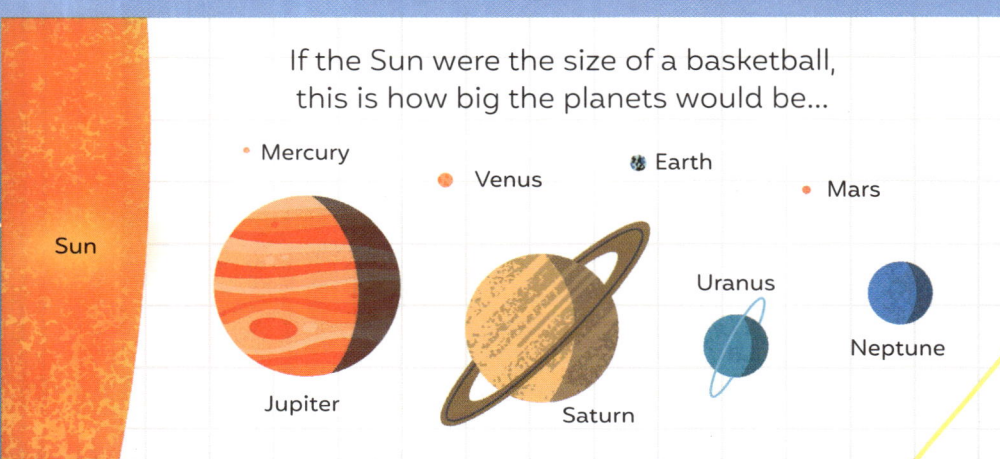

If the Sun were the size of a basketball, this is how big the planets would be…

...and they would be spread over a HUGE area!

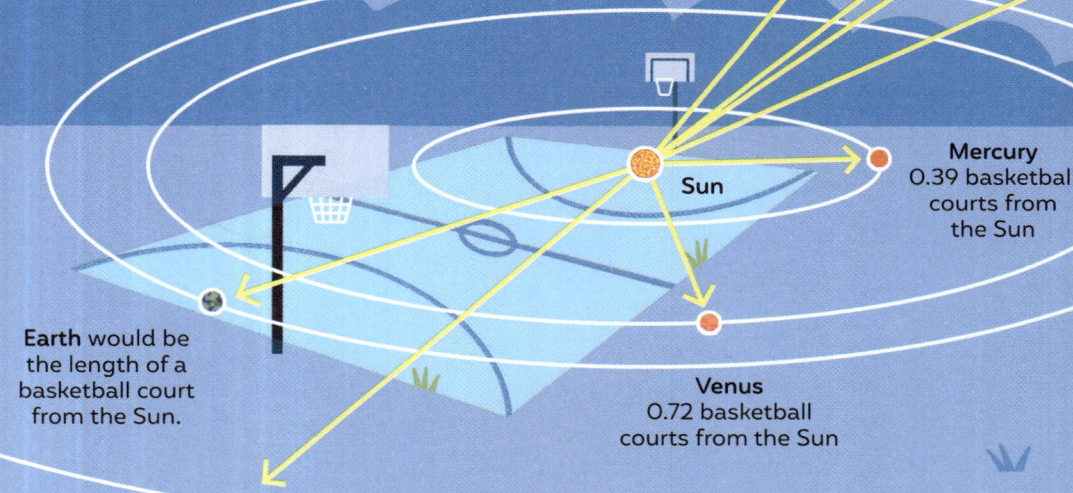

Mercury 0.39 basketball courts from the Sun

Venus 0.72 basketball courts from the Sun

Earth would be the length of a basketball court from the Sun.

Mars 1.5 basketball courts from the Sun

The inner planets are bunched much closer together than the outer ones – though even these planets are millions of miles apart.

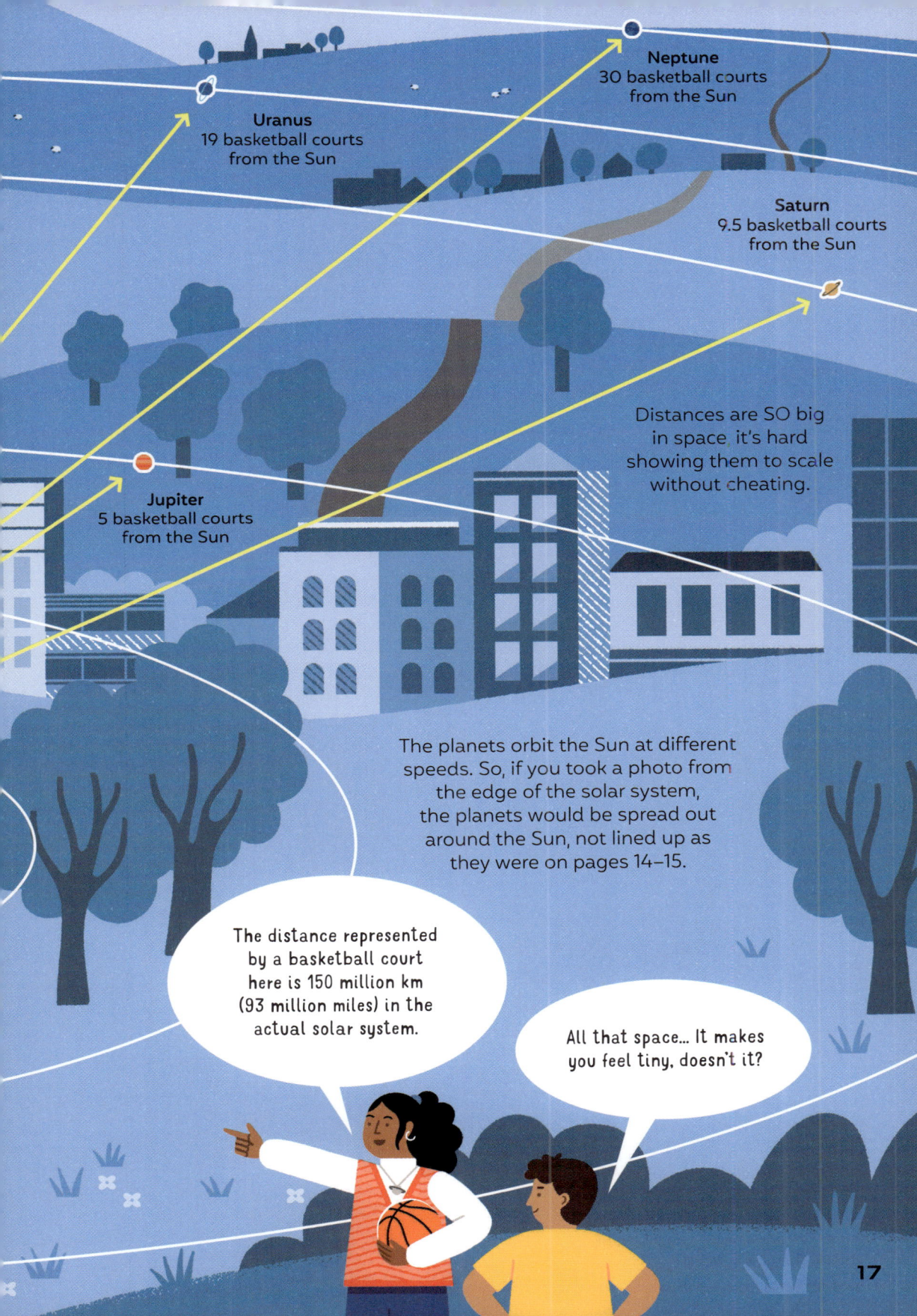

THE SUN

The night sky is dotted with twinkling stars, but there's only one that really matters for OUR lives on Earth – the Sun. It's the heart of the solar system.

Stars are giant, glowing balls of gas – and the Sun is no different. Its core, where its energy is generated, is a scorching 15 million °C (27 million °F). The surface is a *relatively* chilly 5,500°C (10,000°F).

It's a giant anchor, holding Earth, the rest of the whirling planets and all the other stuff in the solar system in orbit around it. This is down to something called **gravity** – you can find out more about that in chapter 6.

But the Sun is moving as well. It orbits the middle of the Milky Way Galaxy, along with around 100 billion other stars.

"Whoa! The Sun must be GIGANTIC. It's so much bigger than those other stars."

"Well, it *is* pretty big – Earth could fit into it over a million times. But there are MUCH bigger stars out there."

"The Sun is our closest. It's far enough away that it looks calm and stable from Earth. In fact, it's chaotic and busy, full of swirling, seething activity."

The Sun releases a constant stream of tiny particles, known as **solar wind**. When solar wind breezes into Earth's atmosphere, beautiful light displays, called auroras, appear in the sky.

Sometimes the Sun spits out bubbles of burning gas, called **coronal mass ejections**. These can interfere with electronics on Earth and in space.

Solar flares are massive explosions of energy. They're so powerful, they can cut off radio communications on Earth.

Aside from these dramatic outbursts, the Sun is also a constant source of heat and light – and that's REALLY important for life on Earth...

19

EARTH: THE PERFECT PLANET?

Earth is the planet we know best. It's also unique – as far as we know, it's the only planet that's home to living things. That's down to a series of astronomical properties that make it ideal for life.

TILT
Around 4.5 BILLION years ago, shortly after Earth formed, it collided with a huge space rock around the size of Mars. This enormous impact knocked Earth over slightly. So, the axis it spins around is tilted as it orbits the Sun.

Due to this tilt, different parts of Earth are exposed to the Sun during Earth's orbit. This is what gives us seasons and prevents extreme temperatures on Earth.

LOCATION
Earth is perfectly positioned to have liquid water – a key requirement for life. If it were further away from the Sun, it would be too cold. If it were closer, too hot. Scientists call this location the **habitable zone**, or **Goldilocks zone** – just like Goldilocks' porridge, Earth's temperature is just right.

ATMOSPHERE

Earth is surrounded by a thick layer of gases, known as its **atmosphere**. This is held in place by Earth's gravity. If Earth was smaller, its atmosphere wouldn't be as thick.

The atmosphere absorbs harmful radiation and protects us from space rocks, which burn up as they pass through it. It also traps heat inside to keep Earth warm and holds the air we breathe.

MAGNETOSPHERE

Earth has an iron core, which makes it behave like a giant magnet. This creates a magnetic force around Earth, known as the **magnetosphere**. It acts as a shield, deflecting dangerous radiation from the Sun.

FIT FOR LIFE

Thanks to its distance from the Sun, the angle of its tilt and its thick atmosphere, Earth has just the right conditions for life.

 Well-regulated temperatures

 Liquid water

 Plentiful sunlight

 Protection from radiation and rocks

Astronomers are on the lookout for OTHER planets that share these properties. They could be home to other life forms.

THE MOON

The Moon is our closest companion in the solar system. It's Earth's only **natural satellite** – that means it's the only natural object in orbit around our planet.

The Moon formed roughly 4.5 billion years ago. Many experts think it emerged from the collision that gave Earth its tilt.

SMASH
CRUNCH

According to this theory, the enormous crash sent chunks of rock flying into space. They eventually clumped together and formed the Moon, which has been circling Earth ever since.

Earth looked very different back then – it was just a ball of molten rock.

If the Moon formed not long after Earth... And is made from the same rocks as Earth... Isn't it basically a mini Earth?

Good question. The Moon doesn't have strong enough gravity to hold a thick atmosphere around it like Earth, so –

So it must have way less protection from space rocks and the Sun's rays. And nothing to trap heat at night.

Exactly! It's a harsh place. The surface is peppered with craters. In the day, temperatures reach 127°C (260°F). At night, they drop to -173°C (-280°F).

GULP. I won't complain about the weather on Earth again.

22

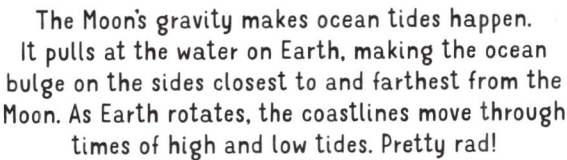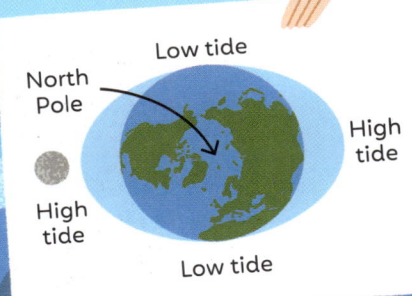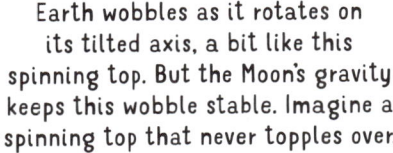

SPACE ROCKS

The Sun, planets and our Moon get a lot of attention, but they aren't the only things in our solar system. There are lots of other objects whizzing around out there.

DWARF PLANETS

These are big rocks that aren't quite big enough to be planets.

They're roughly spherical, so they *look* like planets. But, unlike planets, they're not big enough to clear other objects from their path through space. Pluto is the best known.

COMETS

A bit like big snowballs in space – they are clumps of ice and dust.

When a comet is near to the Sun, the ice in it melts. This produces a big cloud around the comet called a coma, and gives it long, beautiful tails made of dust and gas.

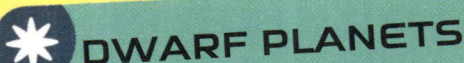 ASTEROIDS

Lumps of rock left over from the formation of the solar system. Also known as minor planets.

The biggest are hundreds of miles wide. The smallest are the size of a house. Most are found in a big ring between Mars and Jupiter, known as the Asteroid Belt.

METEOROIDS

Technically, any rocky object flying through space is a meteoroid. But astronomers usually use the term to refer to objects smaller than asteroids.

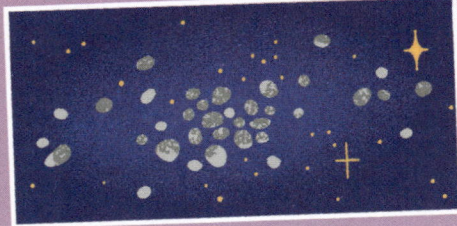

Some are as small as pebbles. They form when bigger objects, such as asteroids or comets, break into smaller chunks.

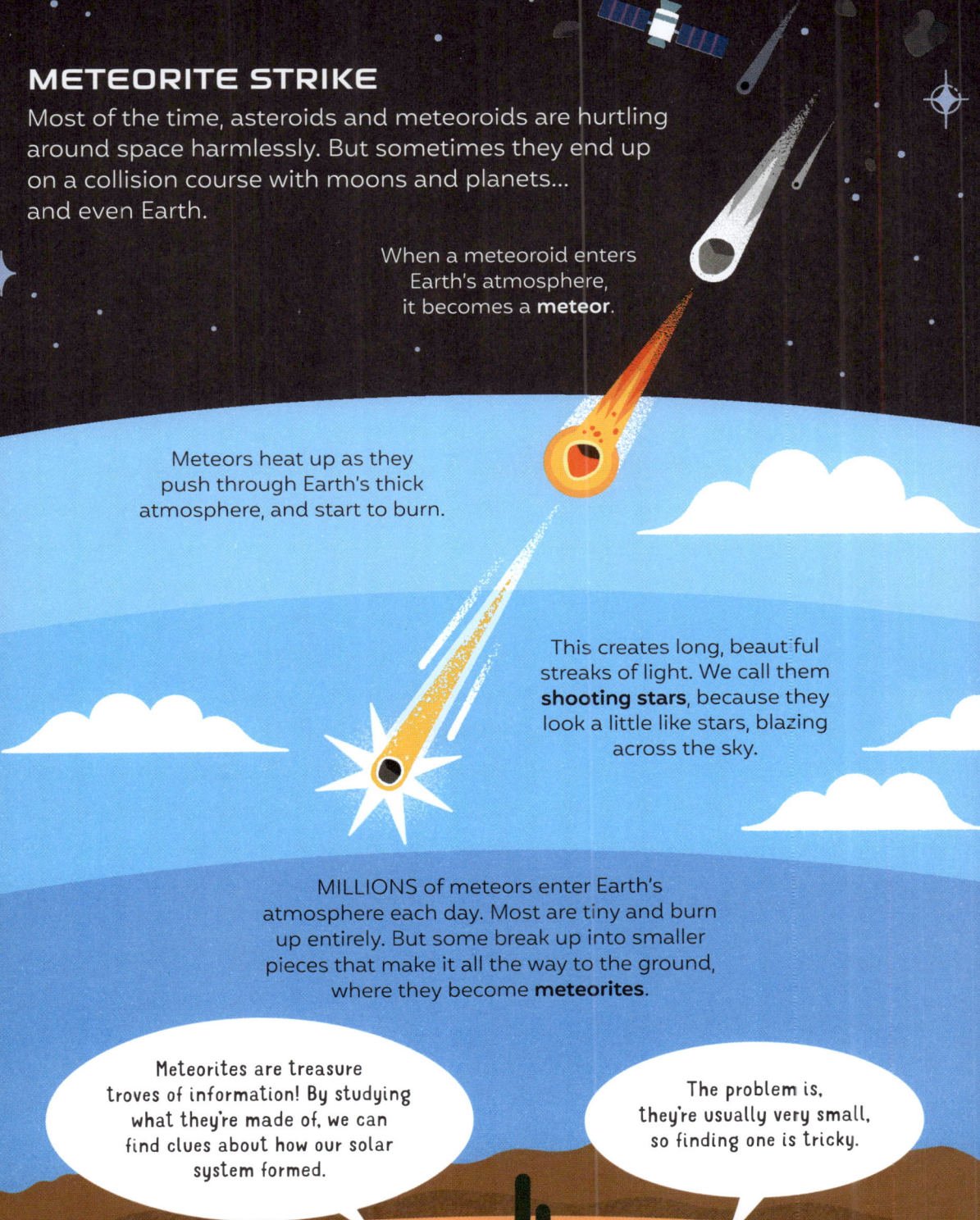

LIFT OFF!

From the 1950s, humans began sending rockets into space. Some carried equipment or astronauts on missions to explore the solar system. Others launched satellites to help us on Earth.

Huge leaps were made in space exploration, as two rival world powers – the USA and the Soviet Union (which had its capital in Moscow, Russia) – raced to show their technological prowess. Here are some key dates.

1957
The Soviet Union launched the first artificial satellite – a human-made object in orbit around Earth. The device was called *Sputnik*.

1961
Yuri Gagarin from the Soviet Union became the first human to blast off into space.

Thousands of satellites have been launched in the years since, by many different countries.

Some transmit radio and television.

Others collect information about the weather...

...or help with GPS location mapping on Earth...

...or even spy on people.

As of 2026, around 650 people have been into space.

Space travel might one day be open to anyone who can afford it.

SPACE-ME
Price: Sorry, more than your lifetime earnings.

1969

US astronauts Neil Armstrong and Buzz Aldrin were the first people to walk on the Moon.

1977

The US launched space probes *Voyager 1* and *Voyager 2*, to explore the entire solar system.

1988

The first part of the International Space Station (ISS) was launched. The station is a collaboration between the US, Russia, Europe, Japan and Canada.

It's a giant leap for mankind!

The Moon is still the most distant place humans have visited.

Astronauts have collected hundreds of Moon rocks.

The ISS has been continually inhabited by astronauts for more than 20 years. We use it as a science lab to conduct experiments in space.

Its mission comes to an end around 2030.

These are very similar to rocks on Earth, supporting the theory that the Moon formed when Earth suffered an almighty crash.

2012

Voyager 1 left the solar system. It is further from the Sun than any other human-made object.

To infinity and beyond...

MAKING A MESS

Humans have launched THOUSANDS of objects into space. Most continue to circle Earth in one form or another. Unfortunately, this has made quite a mess.

Today, more than 11,000 satellites orbit Earth.

Their orbits are carefully set, so they don't collide.

But, alongside these, there are more than 130 MILLION pieces of space junk — remnants of rockets, spacecraft and defunct satellites — whose orbits we can't control.

Some of this space debris is the size of a bus.

It would be a complete disaster if a large piece collided with a spacecraft.

Labs like ours use radar to monitor all the debris large enough to track from Earth — around 35,000 pieces.

Space junk is the single biggest threat to astronauts up in space and the future of space travel.

Part of a radar network monitoring Low Earth Orbit (LEO).

ACCIDENTS WAITING TO HAPPEN

This space junk problem is on the verge of spinning out of control.

Every collision creates MORE space junk...

...increasing the chance of MORE collisions...

...creating EVEN MORE debris, and so on.

Circling Earth at speeds as high as 29,000km (18,000 miles) per hour, even tiny pieces of debris, such as a fleck of paint, can cause significant damage.

In 2016, a piece smaller than a poppy seed chipped one of the ISS's windows.

Unless we find a way to clear up our mess, sending anything up into space will become too risky. If this meant we could no longer rely on satellites, it would affect our lives on Earth, too.

Luckily, scientists around the world are developing lots of clever methods to catch space debris, including nets and suction devices.

ALL WE CAN SEE

People have been stargazing for thousands of years, but their understanding of the universe totally changed when the telescope was invented, 400 years ago. It allowed astronomers to see the night sky in more and more detail.

Nowadays, powerful telescopes on Earth and in space can bring incredibly faint and faraway stars into view. Astronomers have also sent probes to investigate other planets and moons. With their help, we've seen further into the universe than we will probably ever go – and much further than early stargazers could ever have imagined.

SEEING FURTHER, SEEING FAINTER

In a relatively short period of time, telescopes have transformed what astronomers can see.

AROUND 1608

The first telescopes were invented, using glass lenses inside a wooden tube. To start with, they could enlarge images around three times.

Light enters here.

A lens bends the light to focus the image.

Telescopes like this are known as **refracting telescopes**. People still use them today.

The eyepiece lens magnifies the image.

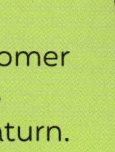

Within a couple of years, telescopes could magnify twenty times – enough for astronomer Galileo Galilei to notice strange, fuzzy parts sticking out from the sides of the planet Saturn.

1655

Christiaan Huygens built a telescope with a much bigger lens that could capture much more light and magnify forty-three times. It made it possible to identify Saturn's sticking-out parts as rings surrounding the planet.

To see further, astronomers would need a bigger telescope to capture even more light. But there's a limit to how big you can build a glass lens, so astronomers started working with mirrors...

1668

Isaac Newton built the first working **reflecting telescope**.

Instead of a glass lens, it used a curved mirror to focus light. Using mirrors opened the way for much larger telescopes, which could collect enough light to see much fainter objects.

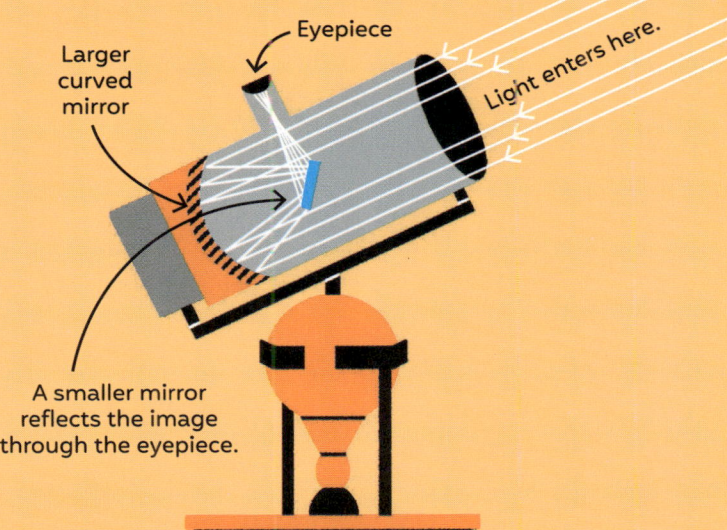

Eyepiece
Larger curved mirror
Light enters here.
A smaller mirror reflects the image through the eyepiece.

1923

Edwin Hubble was using a huge telescope, with a 2.5m (8ft) mirror, to take a close look at a cloud of dust and stars called Andromeda. People thought the Milky Way Galaxy was all there was, and that Andromeda was just part of it. But Hubble showed it was much too far away for this to be true. It was a different galaxy!

Andromeda Galaxy

I showed that the Milky Way was just a tiny part of a MUCH LARGER universe – and that there were other galaxies out there.

At the time, the telescope Hubble used was the largest in the world, but that soon changed...

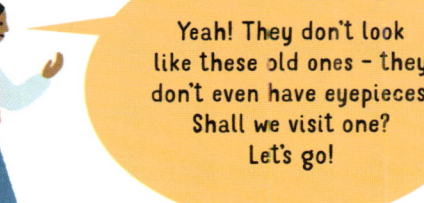

I hear telescopes today are the size of buildings.

Yeah! They don't look like these old ones – they don't even have eyepieces. Shall we visit one? Let's go!

The observatory housing the telescope is ENORMOUS and packed with huge pieces of equipment.

Most impressive is the telescope's 10m (33ft) mirror. It's made from smaller hexagonal mirrors, each worth around 2 million US dollars. Its scale makes it around 10 MILLION times better at gathering light than a human eye.

Some of these devices investigate light from stars and planets by splitting it apart. More on this later...

Additional mirrors help focus the light to make a clear picture.

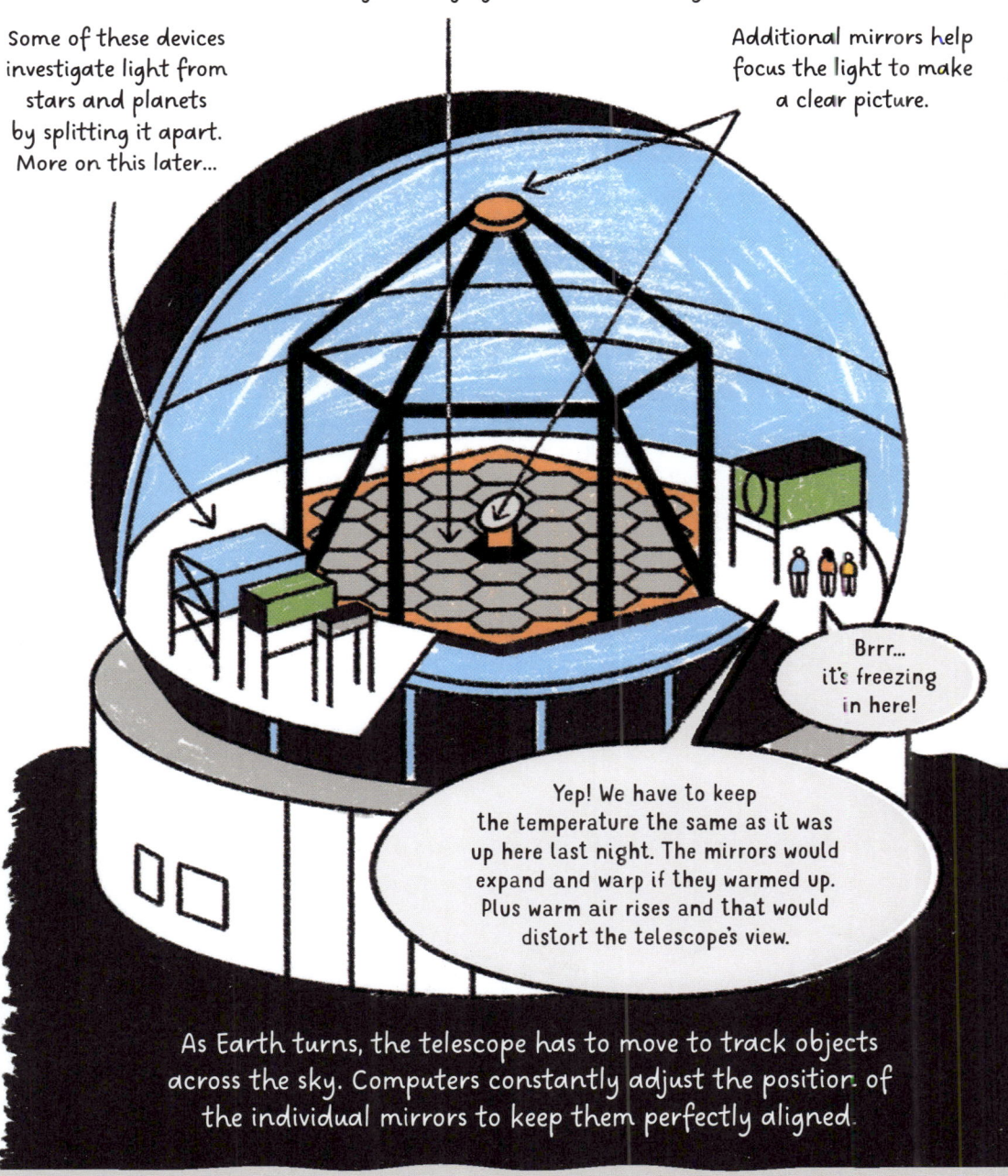

Brrr... it's freezing in here!

Yep! We have to keep the temperature the same as it was up here last night. The mirrors would expand and warp if they warmed up. Plus warm air rises and that would distort the telescope's view.

As Earth turns, the telescope has to move to track objects across the sky. Computers constantly adjust the position of the individual mirrors to keep them perfectly aligned.

BACK AT THE BASE

As the sun set, the roof above the telescope opened, but we were already back at the base...

The telescope and other equipment can be controlled from computers, so astronomers don't need to be nearby.

Using a modern telescope means looking at LOADS of screens.

Say cheese, Kim!

This big screen shows images and information the telescope is gathering. The other computers control devices at the observatory.

Kim Comet, the astronomer we met, thinks there might be a ninth planet in the solar system, around the size of Neptune. She was using the telescope to search for it.

Telescopes like this are INCREDIBLY expensive and there aren't many, so they're always in high demand. Astronomers have to apply to get time on a telescope.

If it rains or snows on the nights you're given, the roof above the telescope stays closed... That's really tough luck.

But when you get a clear view, there are amazing discoveries to be made...

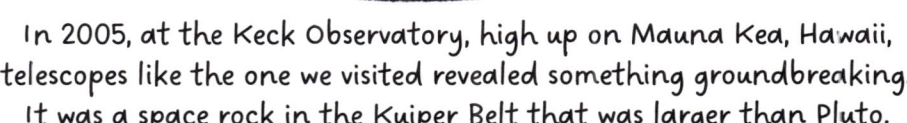

SPOTTED

In 2005, at the Keck Observatory, high up on Mauna Kea, Hawaii, telescopes like the one we visited revealed something groundbreaking. It was a space rock in the Kuiper Belt that was <u>larger</u> than Pluto.

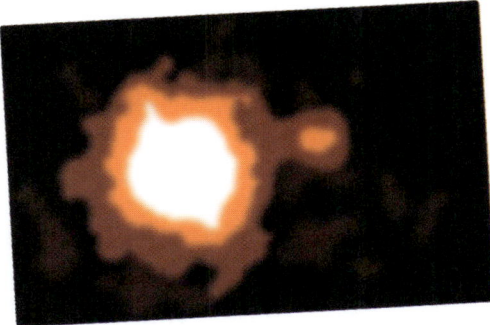

Astronomers named it <u>Eris,</u> after an ancient Greek goddess of strife – as they knew it would cause problems for them.

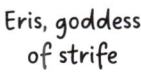

Eris, goddess of strife

Astronomers used to think of Pluto as the solar system's ninth planet. But, when they discovered Eris, they had to rethink that. Pluto became a dwarf planet.

> It was finding Eris that convinced astronomers a planet HAS TO be big enough to have cleared other large space rocks from its orbit.

Also at Keck, astronomers have made images of some of the planets orbiting distant stars.

To do this, telescope images are processed to block the star's light. This makes it possible to see the much fainter light from orbiting planets.

> There's a star called HR 8799 here. Its light has been blocked, revealing four planets circling it.

A BLURRY VIEW

We simply couldn't live without Earth's atmosphere – but sometimes it gets in the way…

Ah, not a cloud in the sky. What a perfect view of space!

If only! We can't see our atmosphere, but it's there – and it actually blurs what we can see a bit. Here, I'll show you.

When light passes through different layers of the atmosphere, it refracts – that's a fancy way of saying it bends.

It's the way the light bends that makes stars appear to twinkle. It's beautiful – but bad if you want to take a sharp picture.

Light pollution from big cities and the faint glow of chemicals in the atmosphere make getting a good picture even harder.

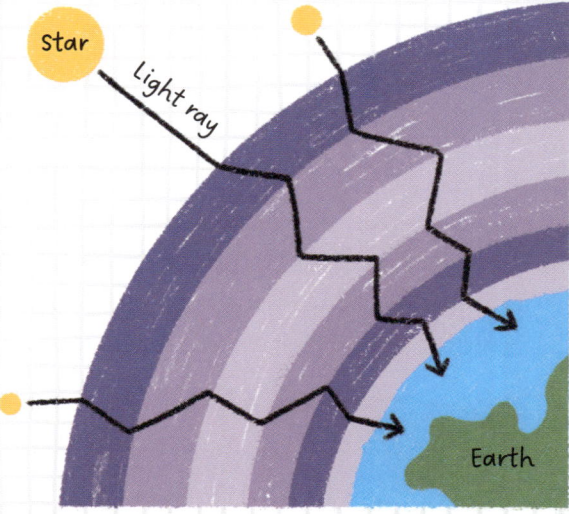

Today, some of the most advanced telescopes on Earth have clever technology to correct for the distorting effects of Earth's atmosphere. But astronomers have found another solution too…

EYES IN THE SKY

To escape the fuzzy effects of Earth's atmosphere, astronomers have sent telescopes into space. Out there, space telescopes take truly astonishing images of the universe. And, unlike telescopes on Earth, they can work non-stop – there's no weather or daytime where they are.

Launched in 1990, the **Hubble Space Telescope** is still hard at work roughly 515km (320 miles) above our heads.

This photograph, taken by Hubble in 2014, is called *Pillars of Creation*. It shows plumes of dust and gas in the Milky Way. Inside them, new stars are forming.

This image, the *Hubble Ultra Deep Field*, shows a mind-blowing 10,000 galaxies in a tiny patch of the sky.

Hubble's camera took this image over several months in 2003 and 2004.

By counting the galaxies in this image, astronomers were able to estimate that there are about 100 BILLION galaxies in the universe.

39

PROBING SPACE

Telescopes aren't the only tools sent out to explore space. Astronomers have sent unpiloted spacecraft, called **space probes**, to EVERY planet in the solar system, as well as to lots of moons, asteroids and comets.

Unlike spacecraft with astronauts on board, it doesn't matter if space probes never return to Earth. In fact, most are designed to beam their findings back to Earth instead.

Flyby probes whiz past their target once.

The *New Horizons* probe flew by Pluto in 2015, nine years after it left Earth. It took pictures and gathered data about Pluto's atmosphere and size.

Orbiter probes enter orbit around their target and stay there.

A probe called *Juno* started orbiting Jupiter in 2016. It has mapped the planet's magnetic field and recorded data about its atmosphere and its structure.

Lander probes land on their target, but don't move once they get there.

In 2005, a probe called *Huygens* landed on Titan, one of Saturn's moons. Its job was to study Titan's atmosphere and surface.

To explore the surface of a planet, moon or other space rock, scientists send probes called **rovers** – robotic vehicles designed to drive around, taking scientific measurements as they go.

One of those rovers, named *Perseverance*, launched in June 2020 and reached Mars just over seven months later, in February 2021.

It's on a mission to search for signs of life that might have existed on Mars billions of years ago.

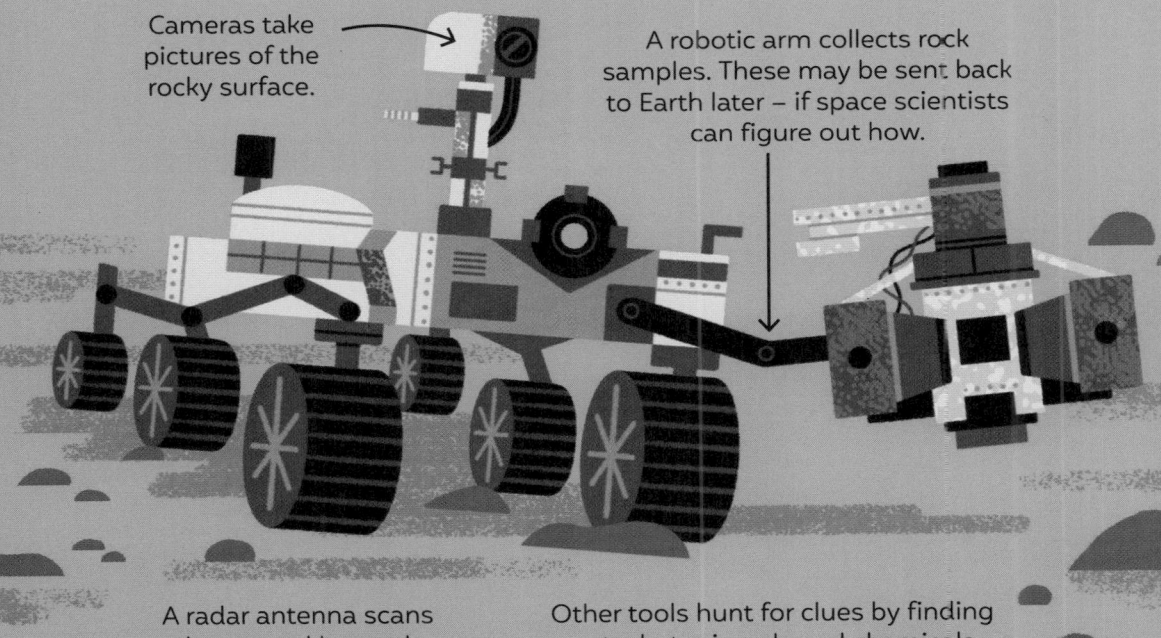

Cameras take pictures of the rocky surface.

A robotic arm collects rock samples. These may be sent back to Earth later – if space scientists can figure out how.

A radar antenna scans the ground beneath the surface.

Other tools hunt for clues by finding out what minerals and chemicals make up rocks on the surface.

Perseverance is trundling around a vast crater that scientists think might have been a lake long ago. This is a good place to search for signs of ancient life forms, since water is the key ingredient for life as we know it.

The data *Perseverance* collects is beamed back to Earth where it's studied for signs of long-lost life.

MORE THAN MEETS THE EYE

There's no question of visiting stars – they're much too hot and far away. But astronomers have learned an enormous amount about them – and other objects in space – just by studying the radiation they give off.

Some of this radiation is visible light, which tells astronomers all kinds of things about stars and other objects in space.

But the majority of it is actually invisible to our eyes. Using fancy telescopes, we can detect this radiation, and gain new views of the universe.

Amazing! Imagine if that's what space really looked like.

Well it is, sort of. We just can't see it like this with our own eyes – we need the help of some clever telescopes...

"This is all really fascinating. But does it have anything to do with astronomy?"

"Yes, I promise! But first we need to understand how waves work. Throw a pebble into that pond."

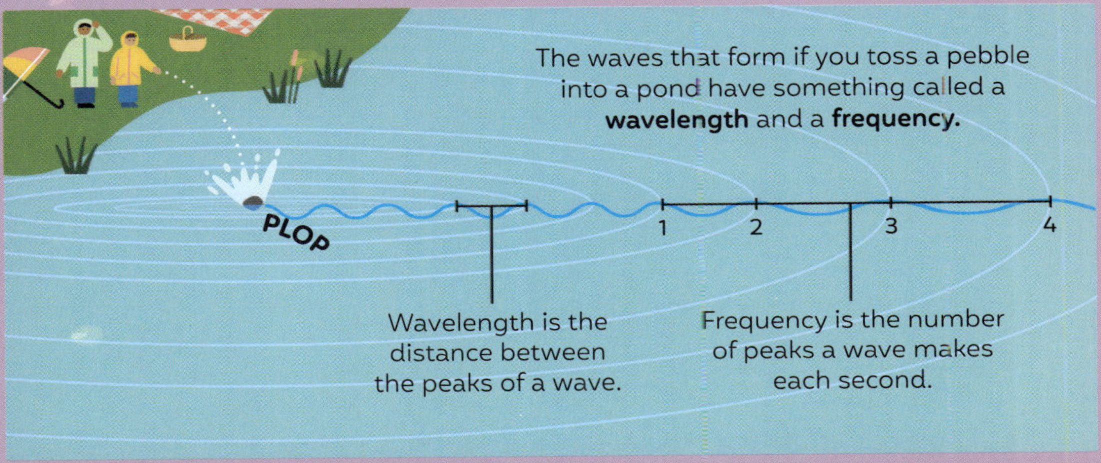

The waves that form if you toss a pebble into a pond have something called a **wavelength** and a **frequency**.

Wavelength is the distance between the peaks of a wave.

Frequency is the number of peaks a wave makes each second.

Light waves are MUCH smaller than water waves, but they have wavelengths and frequencies, too. Each part of the rainbow has a different wavelength and frequency.

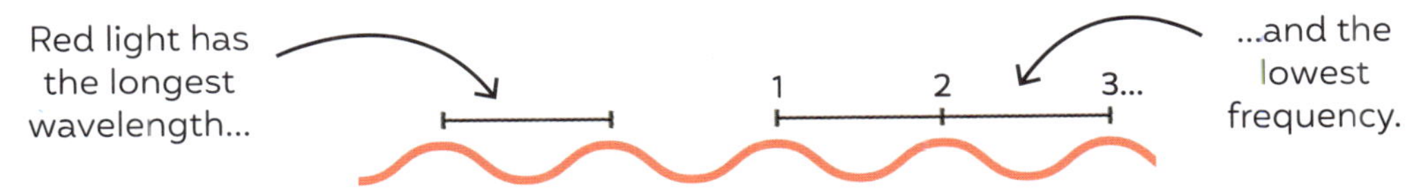

Red light has the longest wavelength... ...and the lowest frequency.

Waves with longer wavelengths have less energy.

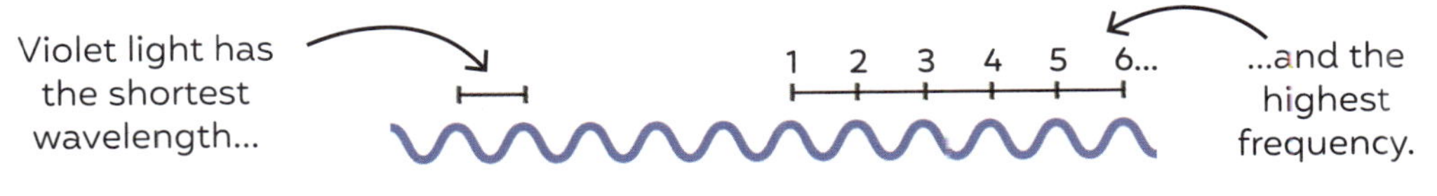

Violet light has the shortest wavelength... ...and the highest frequency.

Waves with shorter wavelengths have more energy.

Knowing the characteristics of different light waves helps astronomers understand what they're looking at in space. In fact, it can tell them far more than they can see with their eyes alone.

45

STUDYING STARS

Light is packed full of information. By looking closely at it, astronomers can gather clues about everything from a star's temperature to the chemicals inside it.

As much as they might want to, astronomers can't travel to stars and prod them with thermometers. Luckily, getting an idea of a star's temperature is as simple as seeing if it's blue, red, or somewhere in between.

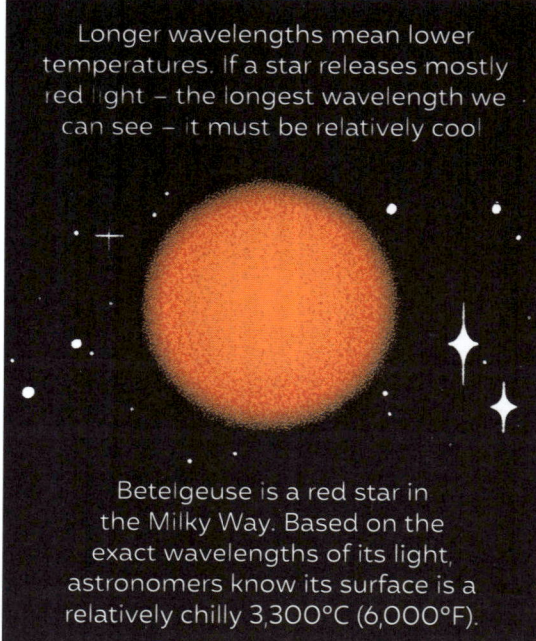

Longer wavelengths mean lower temperatures. If a star releases mostly red light – the longest wavelength we can see – it must be relatively cool

Betelgeuse is a red star in the Milky Way. Based on the exact wavelengths of its light, astronomers know its surface is a relatively chilly 3,300°C (6,000°F).

If a star releases mostly blue light – which has a much shorter wavelength – it must be relatively hot.

Rigel, another star in the Milky Way, is bright blue. Its wavelengths tell us it has a scorching hot surface, somewhere around 12,000°C (21,500°F).

Our closest star, the Sun, emits lots of yellow light.

So, because yellow is between red and blue in the rainbow, its temperature must be somewhere between that of Betelgeuse and Rigel.

That's right! The Sun's surface is about 5,500°C (10,000°F).

To find out about the chemicals inside a star, astronomers use technology to study its light in greater detail.

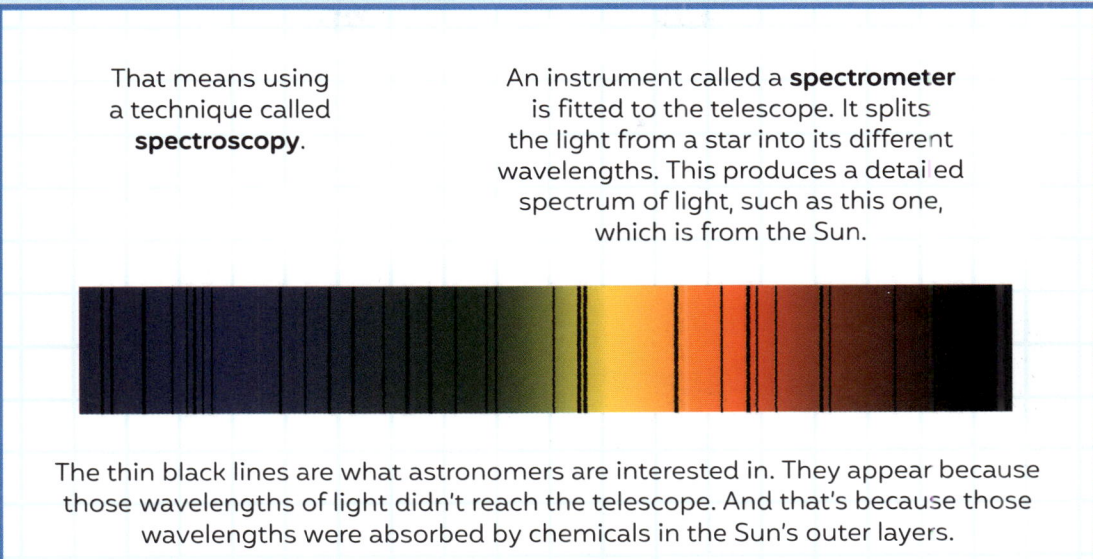

That means using a technique called **spectroscopy**.

An instrument called a **spectrometer** is fitted to the telescope. It splits the light from a star into its different wavelengths. This produces a detailed spectrum of light, such as this one, which is from the Sun.

The thin black lines are what astronomers are interested in. They appear because those wavelengths of light didn't reach the telescope. And that's because those wavelengths were absorbed by chemicals in the Sun's outer layers.

Through lab testing, astronomers know which chemicals absorb which wavelengths. So, they can figure out which chemicals are in the star.

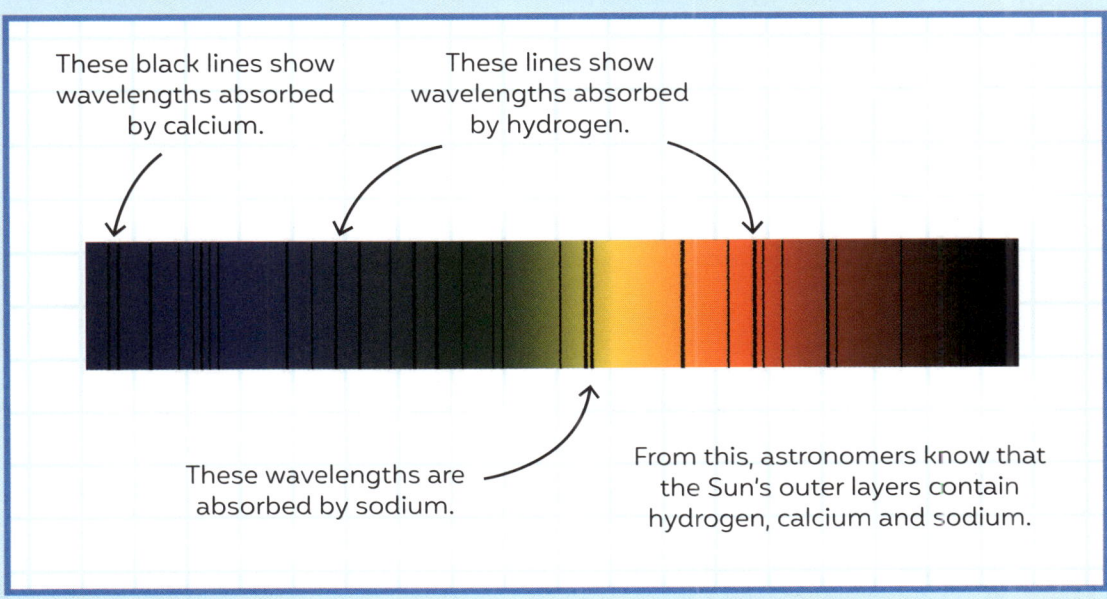

These black lines show wavelengths absorbed by calcium.

These lines show wavelengths absorbed by hydrogen.

These wavelengths are absorbed by sodium.

From this, astronomers know that the Sun's outer layers contain hydrogen, calcium and sodium.

It's an amazingly useful fact that different types of chemicals, known as **elements**, absorb or reflect specific wavelengths of light.

ALL WE CAN'T SEE

In 1800, an astronomer named William Herschel made a mind-blowing discovery. He found that, apart from the light we *can* see, there are waves of light our eyes *can't* detect.

Herschel had set up an experiment to see if all parts of the visible spectrum were the same temperature.

He placed a glass prism in the path of sunlight falling on his table.

Like a raindrop, a prism bends light, separating it out into a rainbow.

He then measured the temperature of different parts of the visible spectrum.

The results showed that temperatures *do* vary across the visible spectrum. But he also discovered something much more unexpected...

Herschel placed a thermometer just beyond the red end of the spectrum, to make sure there wasn't anything else heating up the table. He expected this thermometer to remain at room temperature.

What?! The area just beyond the red end of the spectrum is the hottest of all.

There must be some sort of INVISIBLE LIGHT heating it!

Just like that, Herschel had stumbled upon an entirely new type of light known as **infrared**. And the discoveries didn't stop there...

In fact, the visible spectrum is just a small part of a much broader range of "invisible light" waves, known as the **electromagnetic spectrum**. The universe is flooded with radiation from all parts of this spectrum. You've probably heard of some parts of it, as we use them on Earth for all sorts of things.

Longest wavelength, lowest frequency and energy

Radio waves

The longest wavelengths come from cold clouds of gas.

Microwaves

Infrared

Colder stars emit more infrared light.

Visible light

The light we can see is just a tiny part of the electromagnetic spectrum.

Ultraviolet

Hot, recently formed stars produce lots of ultraviolet light.

X-rays

The shortest wavelengths come from the hottest objects in space, such as scorching clouds of gas and exploding stars.

Gamma rays

Shortest wavelength, highest frequency and energy

All the waves in the electromagnetic spectrum travel at the SAME speed – 299,792,458m (983,600,000ft) per second. They're the fastest thing in the entire universe.

We can't SEE the invisible parts of the spectrum, but we can DETECT them. This opens up a whole new realm of information from the universe...

MAKING PICTURES

Telescopes that detect invisible rays are only helpful if astronomers can turn the information they gather into something we can actually understand. Here's how that works.

First, the telescope gathers data about the rays that reach it. Then, it sends the data to Earth as streams of 0s and 1s, known as binary code.

Powerful computers then convert this jumble of digits into simple black and white images.

Lots of black and white images are then combined to form a more detailed picture.

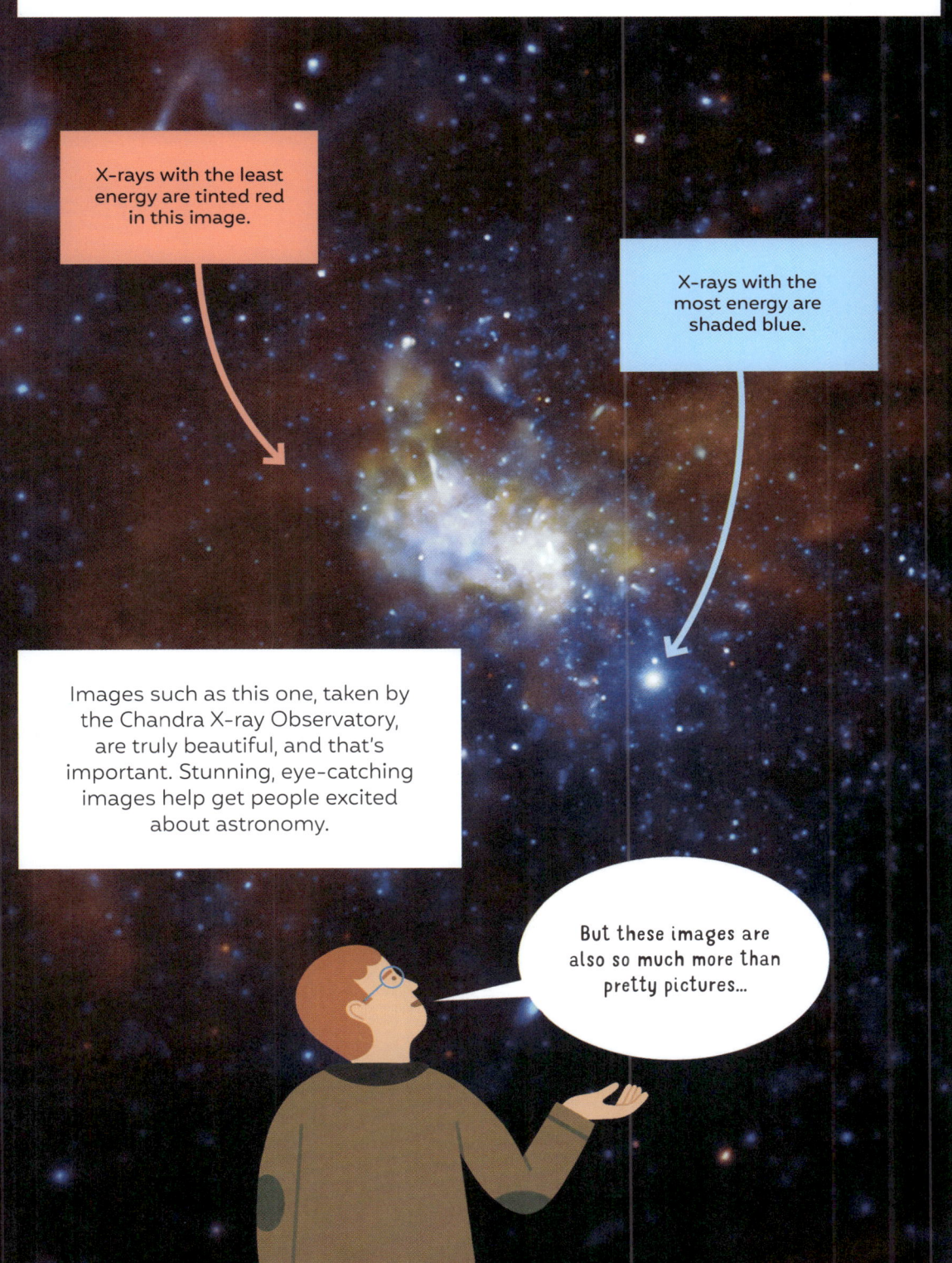

SEEING THE UNSEEABLE

So what do images from the different parts of the electromagnetic spectrum actually tell us? Take a look at these four images of Venus – each taken using light from a different part of the spectrum.

This photo was taken using a camera that's only sensitive to **visible light**. It doesn't tell us much about the planet – other than that it's surrounded by a thick layer of clouds that we can't see through.

This image, taken using a camera sensitive to **ultraviolet light**, reveals those clouds and their contents in more detail.

A gas called sulfur dioxide absorbs some wavelengths of ultraviolet radiation coming from the Sun. So, the image looks darker where there are clouds with lots of this gas.

This helps astronomers understand how winds move clouds around Venus's atmosphere.

"This infrared image shows us how hot Venus's clouds are."

Sensors pick up **infrared** radiating off Venus. Dark red parts of the image show clouds with the lowest temperatures.

White areas show the highest temperatures, which are around Venus's South Pole.

Radio waves pierce through Venus's thick atmosphere to give astronomers a view of the planet's surface.

This image was made by beaming radio waves at Venus and timing how long they take to bounce back. This reveals the texture of the planet's surface.

"Pink areas show towering mountains. Purple areas show deep craters. It looks a bit like Earth, doesn't it?"

LIGHT-YEARS

In space, light – both visible and invisible – doesn't just show us what's out there. It's also the measuring stick astronomers use to gauge the vast distances in the universe.

That's Proxima Centauri, our closest star after the Sun.

How close is it?

It's 40 trillion km (25.3 quadrillion miles) away.

But that's not close at all!

Not by Earth standards, no... There are stars in the universe that are literally BILLIONS of times further away.

To make these huge distances easier to understand, astronomers measure them in a unit known as **light-years**. So, Proxima Centauri is just 4.3 light-years away.

A **light-year** is the distance light travels in a year. And, as light is the fastest thing in the universe, that's a LONG way.

1 light-year = 9,460,000,000,000km (5,880,000,000,000 miles)

For shorter space distances, astronomers sometimes use **light-hours** (the distance light travels in an hour) or **light-minutes** (the distance light travels in a minute).

1 light-hour = 1,080,000,000km (671,000,000 miles)

1 light-minute = 17,990,000km (11,180,000 miles)

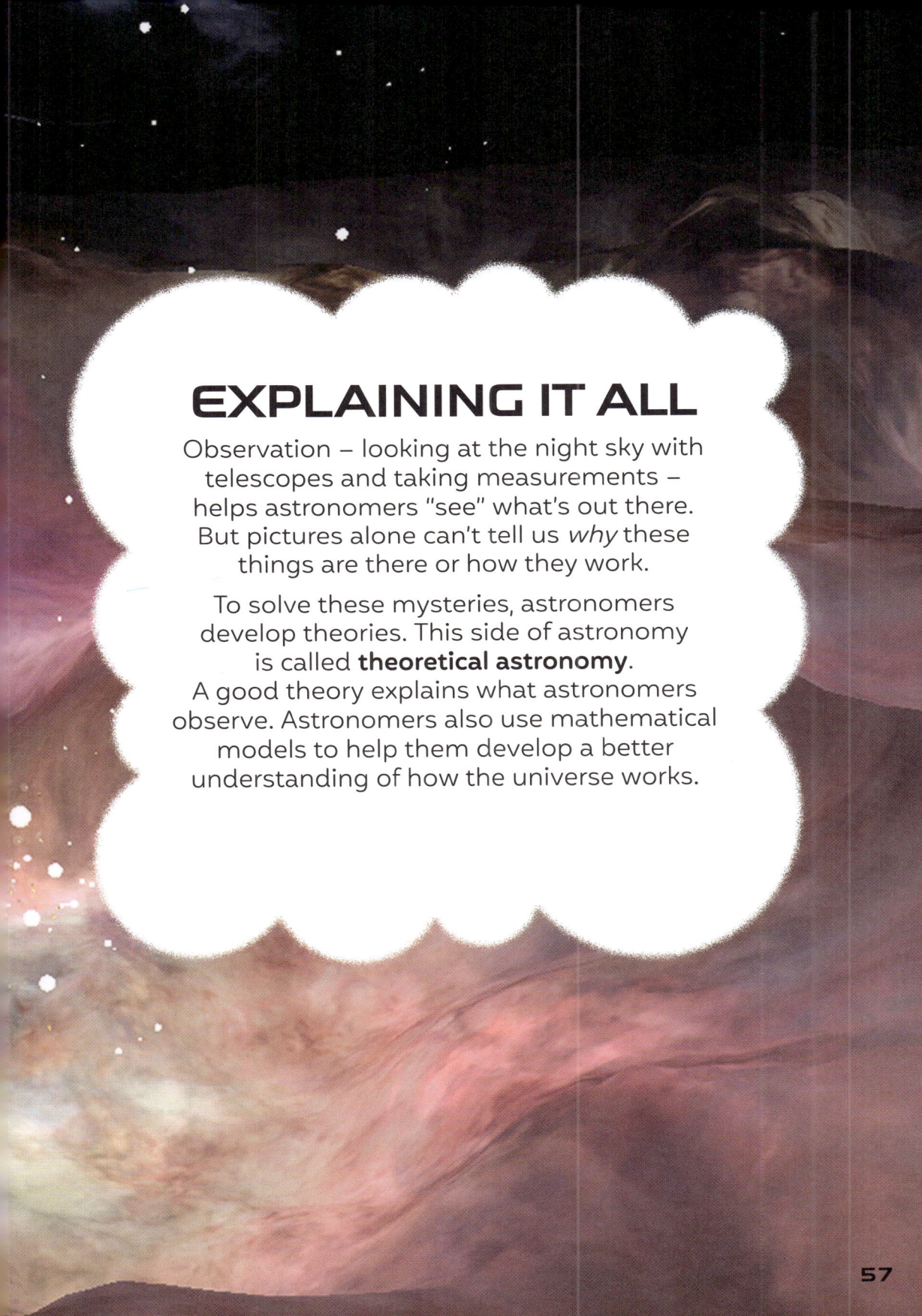

EXPLAINING IT ALL

Observation – looking at the night sky with telescopes and taking measurements – helps astronomers "see" what's out there. But pictures alone can't tell us *why* these things are there or how they work.

To solve these mysteries, astronomers develop theories. This side of astronomy is called **theoretical astronomy**. A good theory explains what astronomers observe. Astronomers also use mathematical models to help them develop a better understanding of how the universe works.

THE LIFE OF STARS

Astronomers come up with theories about how EVERYTHING in the universe works. This diagram shows how stars form, live and die, according to the latest theories.

Astronomers think **baby stars** form gradually over millions of years, in large clouds of dust and hydrogen gas. Gravity pulls hydrogen and dust into clumps.

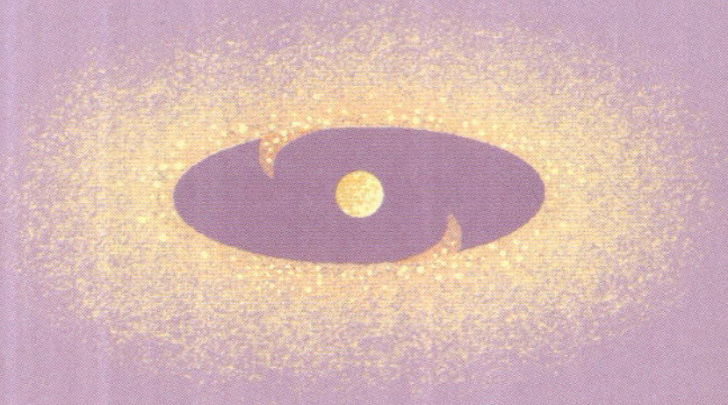

Baby star

As baby stars get bigger, their gravity gets stronger and they become hotter. If they heat up enough, they start to shine, becoming something called a **true star.**

True star

Deep inside a true star, a chemical called hydrogen is heated and squashed so much by the star's gravity that it fuses to become a different chemical called helium.

Hydrogen

Helium

This process is called **fusion.** It releases a HUGE amount of heat and light energy.

If a baby star doesn't grow big enough to become a **true star**, it's known as a failed star, or **brown dwarf**. These are bigger than the biggest planets, but smaller than stars. They give off faint light and heat.

Brown dwarf

Stars shine for millions of years or longer. But eventually, every star starts to run out of hydrogen.

Bigger stars shine brighter, are hotter and run out of hydrogen faster.

In the biggest stars, helium fuses to make other chemicals, including...

 Carbon   Iron   Oxygen   Neon   Silicon

This is how almost every single chemical element in the universe was originally made.

 Smaller stars shine dimmer, cooler and for longer.

Smaller stars fuse helium to make carbon. Then, they puff up and slowly shed their outer layers in an expanding cloud of dust and gas.

The core left behind is known as a **white dwarf**.

This is what will happen to the Sun in about 5 billion years.

Then, gravity makes the star shrink and get even hotter. Eventually, it explodes in something called a **supernova**, spraying these chemicals across the universe.

The star's core is left behind, and crushes down under its own gravity to form a small, but incredibly heavy, star called a **neutron star**. It's far heavier and hotter than a white dwarf.

Whichever path a star follows, it takes billions of years – sometimes even TRILLIONS. No one lives long enough to observe an entire cycle for one star.

How do we know all this if we've never seen the whole life cycle of a star? Are astronomers just making it up?

Kind of... astronomers call it coming up with a theory.

THE THEORY OF STARS

Astronomers didn't come up with the theories to explain stars all at once. It took centuries. Early theories were replaced by better ones as astronomers learned more about the universe.

People used to think that the Sun made its heat and light energy by burning fuel – as if it were a massive lump of coal in the sky.

Then scientists realized that such a ferocious fire would have guzzled up its fuel. If this were happening, the Sun would noticeably reduce in size and give off less heat. But it wasn't shrinking, so they came up with new ideas.

Maybe its supply of fuel is constantly topped up by asteroids hitting it.

Hmm... But we haven't seen many asteroids hitting the Sun.

The Sun must have some other way of making heat and light...

In 1854, German physicist Hermann von Helmholtz argued that the Sun's energy came from its huge gravity causing it to shrink and heat up over time.

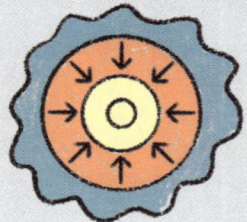

Astronomers liked this idea – and it's partially true. But in the 1920s, I noticed a problem...

British astronomer, Arthur Eddington

If the Sun and other stars were generating all that heat and light through the effects of gravity alone, we'd have noticed them shrinking.

60

In 1905, German physicist Albert Einstein came up with a brilliant idea which he described as **E=mc²**. His theory linked energy (**E**) and mass (**m**). Mass is the scientific word for the amount of "stuff" in something. **c** is the speed of light, 299,792,458m (983,600,000 feet) per second.

Basically, mass can become energy, and energy can become mass. My equation explains that the energy in an object is equal to its mass multiplied by the speed of light squared. **Squared** means "multiplied by itself", so c^2 – and the amount of energy released – is ENORMOUS.

Astronomers didn't understand it yet, but **E=mc²** actually explains how stars work.

Then, in 1925, British-American astronomer Cecilia Payne-Gaposchkin studied the Sun's light. She worked out from the Sun's spectrum that it was almost entirely made of hydrogen and helium.

In the 1930s, scientists discovered that a chemical could undergo fusion and become a completely new one, releasing lots of energy at the same time. That's when they noticed this must be what was happening in stars – hydrogen was fusing to produce helium.

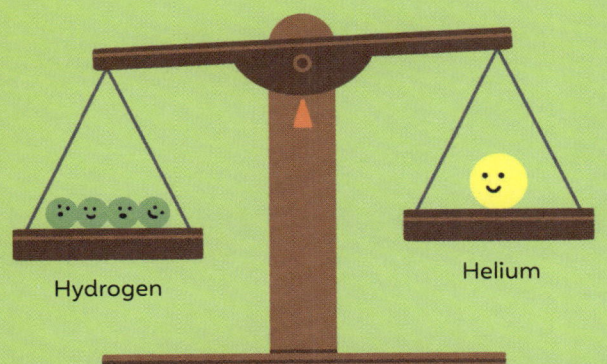

It takes four hydrogen atoms to make a helium atom. When hydrogen fuses into helium, a tiny bit of mass is lost. That lost mass becomes a HUGE amount of energy – just as Einstein's E=mc² theory predicted.

PROVING EVERYTHING

Anyone can come up with a theory. But for it to be accepted, astronomers need to be convinced that it actually describes what's going on. Here are some of the main ways they find proof.

LOOKING FOR EVIDENCE

Astronomers can use telescopes to look for evidence that a theory is correct.

In the 1960s, astronomers predicted the existence of brown dwarfs – baby stars too small to fuse hydrogen into helium, as true stars do.

Now we need to find one... That would show we've really *understood what makes a star blaze into life.*

It took a while. Brown dwarfs are MUCH cooler and fainter than true stars, which makes them tricky to detect. Finally, in 1995, astronomers detected one with the Hubble Space Telescope.

WOO-HOO!

Much later, it turned out that the one they found was actually TWO brown dwarfs, circling each other. Together, they were brighter, which made them easier to spot.

Astronomers have discovered lots more brown dwarfs since. But these discoveries have raised new questions...

Why are some much larger and dimmer than our theories suggest they should be? We still need to figure this out.

LAB EXPERIMENTS

Another way is to carry out experiments in a lab. Astronomers can create environments in the lab that mimic conditions in space – such as extreme temperatures or high levels of radiation – and test whether chemicals behave as their theories predict.

Scientists have heated tiny fragments of iron to millions of degrees.

At this temperature, the iron absorbed more heat than scientists had expected.

This experiment helps explain why heat travels very slowly from deep inside the Sun to its surface. It's because iron in the Sun holds on to the heat.

THOUGHT EXPERIMENTS

Sometimes, theories can be tested simply by imagining a situation and thinking through the consequences. This is called a **thought experiment**.

For instance, 2,000 years ago, people thought the universe was contained within a wall of stars. Roman philosopher Lucretius wasn't so sure.

I imagined running and throwing a javelin at the wall.

If the javelin hits the wall and bounces back, that means there must be something beyond "the universe" that the javelin is bouncing off.

If the javelin pierces the wall, the wall isn't a proper boundary, and the universe continues beyond it.

Either way, there's something beyond what we've been calling "the universe".

Nowadays, we don't think of the universe as having a solid edge, but astronomers are still unsure whether or not it continues forever.

MAKING MODELS

Today, the main way astronomers develop and test theories is by making a **mathematical model**. That's a way of thinking about how stuff in the universe behaves using equations, such as E=mc².

Like a thought experiment, a mathematical model sets up a scenario, then works through the consequences. In the case of a model, astronomers enter data and see what happens.

Once upon a time, seeing what happened meant astronomers making tricky calculations.

Gas naturally spreads out, but gravity can pull it together. How strong does gravity have to be for gas to hold together and form a star?

I'd better keep this model simple... The calculations take AGES and it's easy to make mistakes.

Nowadays, astronomers often use extremely powerful supercomputers to help. These carry out thousands of trillions of calculations per second. And, as long as the calculations and data are entered correctly, the computers never make a mistake.

1.989×10^{30} kg

$\frac{Du}{Dt} = -\nabla w + g$

$\nabla \cdot u = 0$

$\frac{Du}{Dt} = \frac{1}{\rho} \nabla \cdot \sigma + f.$

2.67×10^{27} kg

Supercomputers are SO quick and accurate that we can build really complicated models that come much closer to reflecting the complex reality of the universe.

Another advantage of supercomputer models is that they can produce images and videos as they work through different scenarios.

These supercomputer images show the planets forming within a flat disk of dust and gas swirling around a star.

The entire universe began as an unimaginably tiny point, smaller than the head of a pin.

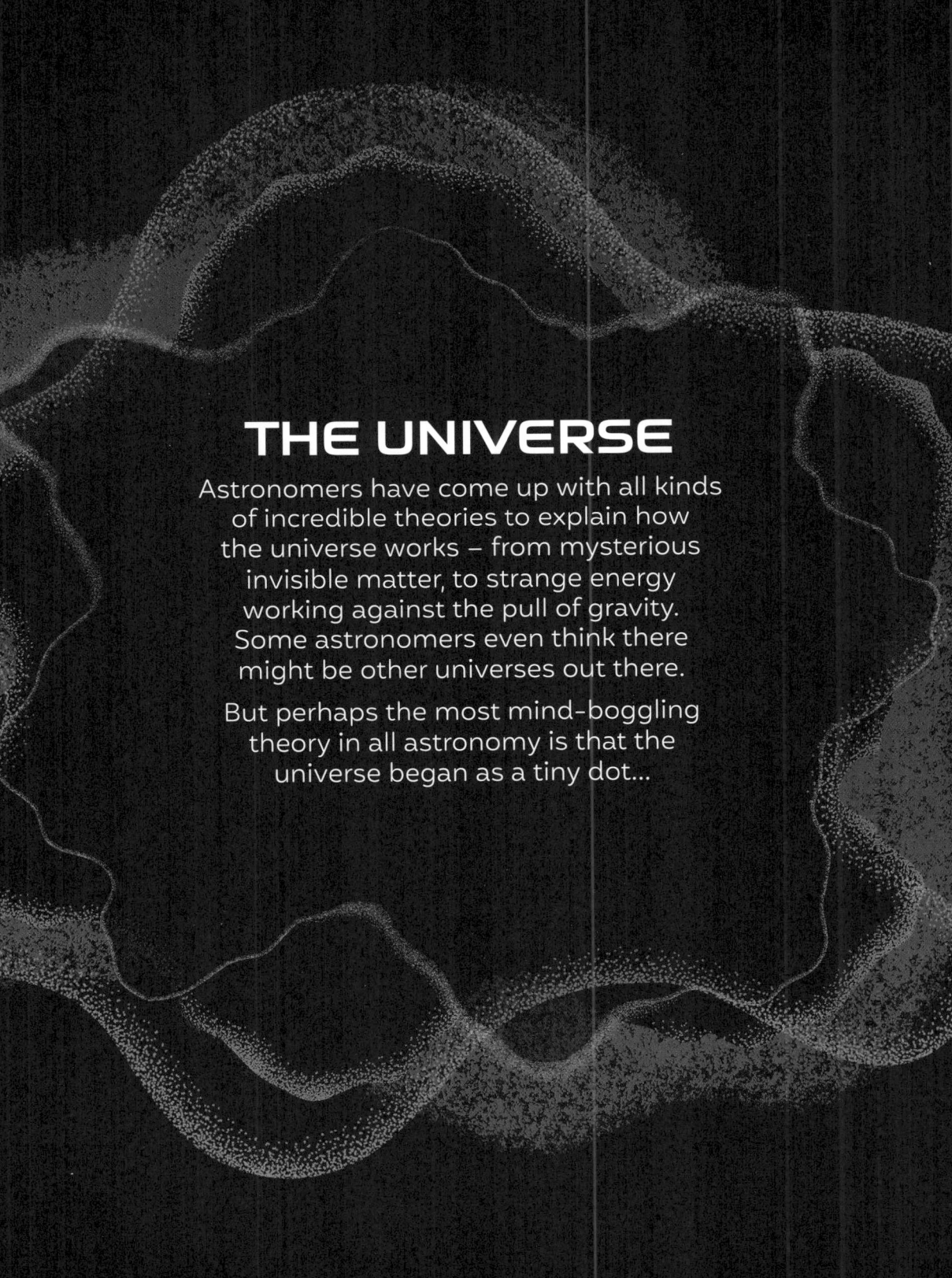

THE UNIVERSE

Astronomers have come up with all kinds of incredible theories to explain how the universe works – from mysterious invisible matter, to strange energy working against the pull of gravity. Some astronomers even think there might be other universes out there.

But perhaps the most mind-boggling theory in all astronomy is that the universe began as a tiny dot...

IN THE BEGINNING...

Most astronomers agree that the best way to explain how all the matter (stuff), space and time we call "the universe" came into being is by a theory called the **Big Bang**. Here's how the theory goes.

The universe, was much, MUCH smaller than this dot. And it was very, VERY dense.

At first, ALL energy and matter was crammed into an unbelievably tiny, extremely hot point. Astronomers call it the **singularity**.

Then, the Big Bang happened. It wasn't actually an explosion, as the name suggests, because there wasn't any space for the universe to explode into.

Instead, it was a period of extremely fast *expansion*. The universe itself started **stretching** out in all directions, creating space and time.

In a mere fraction of a second, it expanded beyond the size of an ENTIRE galaxy.

One second after the Big Bang, the basic building blocks of EVERYTHING – tiny particles called protons, electrons and neutrons – started to form.

STRETCHING OUT

The Big Bang theory isn't just a good story. Clues that it really happened are hidden in the stars – if you look closely enough...

When we look at light from distant stars, it looks more red than we'd expect.

Umm... How do you know the stars aren't just... RED?

Well, we know which elements make up stars. But when we look at the spectra from DISTANT stars, the light absorbed by these elements is shifted to the RED end of the spectrum.

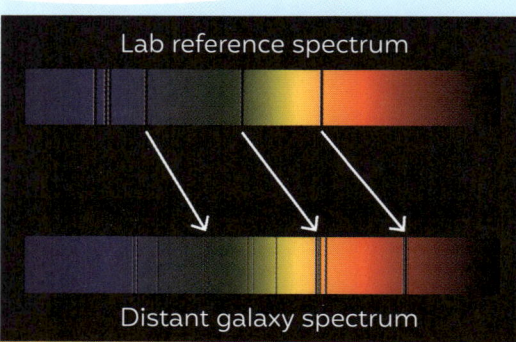

Lab reference spectrum

Distant galaxy spectrum

Huh? I only understand about three of the words you just said...

See how this accordion is all bunched up? There's not much distance between the folds.

Umm, OK... Are you going to play us a song?

70

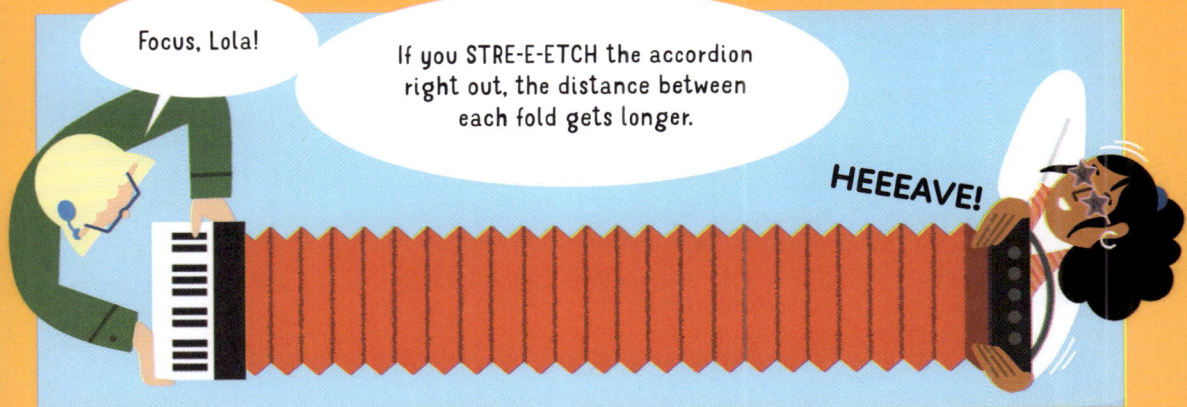

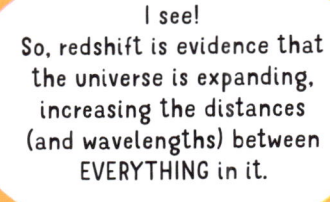

"SEEING" THE BIG BANG

By figuring out how far away galaxies are, and how quickly they're moving away from us, astronomers have calculated that the Big Bang happened around 13.9 BILLION years ago. Incredibly, we can STILL see its effects today.

In 1964, two astronomers, Arno Penzias and Robert Wilson, were studying the skies with a radio telescope. To their annoyance, they noticed the telescope was picking up a constant background noise in the microwave part of the spectrum. They tried everything they could to get rid of it.

No matter what they tried, the background noise persisted. It turned out the telescope wasn't faulty – it was detecting radiation from the Big Bang.

Astronomers call this leftover energy the **cosmic microwave background**, or the **CMB**. Since its accidental discovery, they've used high-tech telescopes to take a closer look.

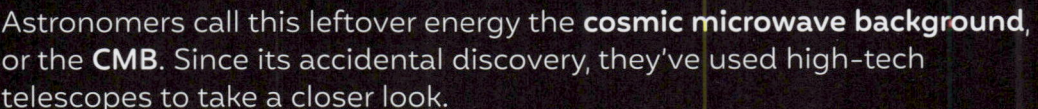

Planck space telescope

The Planck space telescope gathered data between 2009 and 2013 to produce the image below – a map of the CMB across the entire universe.

It shows the FIRST light from the universe, which appeared about 380,000 years after the Big Bang.

The red parts of the image are warmer than the blue areas – but only a TINY bit.

According to the Big Bang theory, the universe expanded and cooled down evenly in all directions. That's exactly what this map of the CMB shows us.

73

DARK MATTER

Gravity, the pull that all matter has, holds galaxies together. But some galaxies appear to have much stronger gravity than their matter alone should generate.

Astronomers first noticed this around a hundred years ago, when they looked at large spinning galaxies, like this one.

These galaxies were spinning too fast for the amount of matter (and therefore gravity) they had – so fast that they should be falling apart. But they weren't.

Huh? We've missed something in our model. The REAL galaxy isn't spinning apart. It must have a LOT of extra gravity coming from something.

RUNNING GALAXY MODEL

WARNING: GALAXY'S GRAVITY TOO LOW... GALAXY SPINNING APART!!!

Astronomers call the mystery source of extra gravity **dark matter**. And they've calculated that there's a LOT of it. The universe seems to contain about five times more dark matter than ordinary matter.

We think dark matter surrounds these galaxies. It's the dark matter's gravity that stops the galaxies from spinning apart.

Dark matter

DEFYING GRAVITY?

In 1998, another discovery shook up our understanding of how the universe works. It was all thanks to the Hubble Space Telescope, which helps astronomers measure distances in the universe.

Astronomers used Hubble to look at the brightness of dying stars. They compared ones in distant galaxies with similar ones in our galaxy, the Milky Way.

Doing this allowed astronomers to calculate how far away these dying stars were.

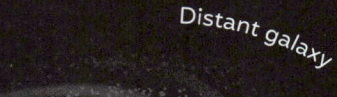

Distant galaxy

Dying star

Milky Way

In 1998, years of analysis revealed that the light from these distant stars was getting fainter. What's more, the light was getting dimmer FASTER AND FASTER over time.

This was a big, big discovery. It could only mean one thing...

Dying star

DAILY NEWS

THE UNIVERSE ISN'T JUST EXPANDING — IT'S EXPANDING AT A FASTER AND FASTER RATE

Incredible discovery earns astronomers Nobel Prize for physics

The prestigious award is shared by Saul Perlmutter, Brian P. Schmidt and Adam G. Riess.

This discovery was extraordinary – and baffling. From their calculations and models, astronomers had expected that the universe's expansion would be slowing by now. They thought the pull of gravity from all the matter and dark matter in the universe should have slowed it down.

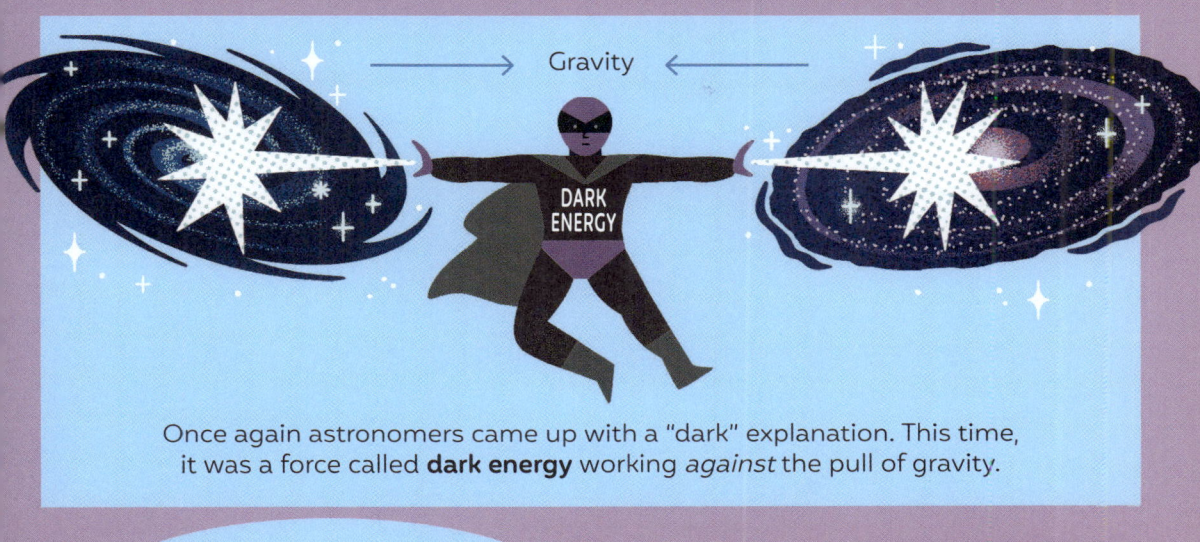

Once again astronomers came up with a "dark" explanation. This time, it was a force called **dark energy** working *against* the pull of gravity.

Dark matter and now dark energy... Is this a joke?

Dark energy does sound like something from the movies – but it isn't a joke.

We don't know much about it at all, but most astronomers *do* think it's the reason why the universe is expanding at an accelerating rate.

I guess we have to suspend our disbelief – at least until we find out more.

Anyway, lots of theories in astronomy seem a bit far-fetched until there's more proof...

THE FATE OF THE UNIVERSE?

Most astronomers agree the universe started with a Big Bang, but what will happen at the end of the universe? Here are the likeliest theories...

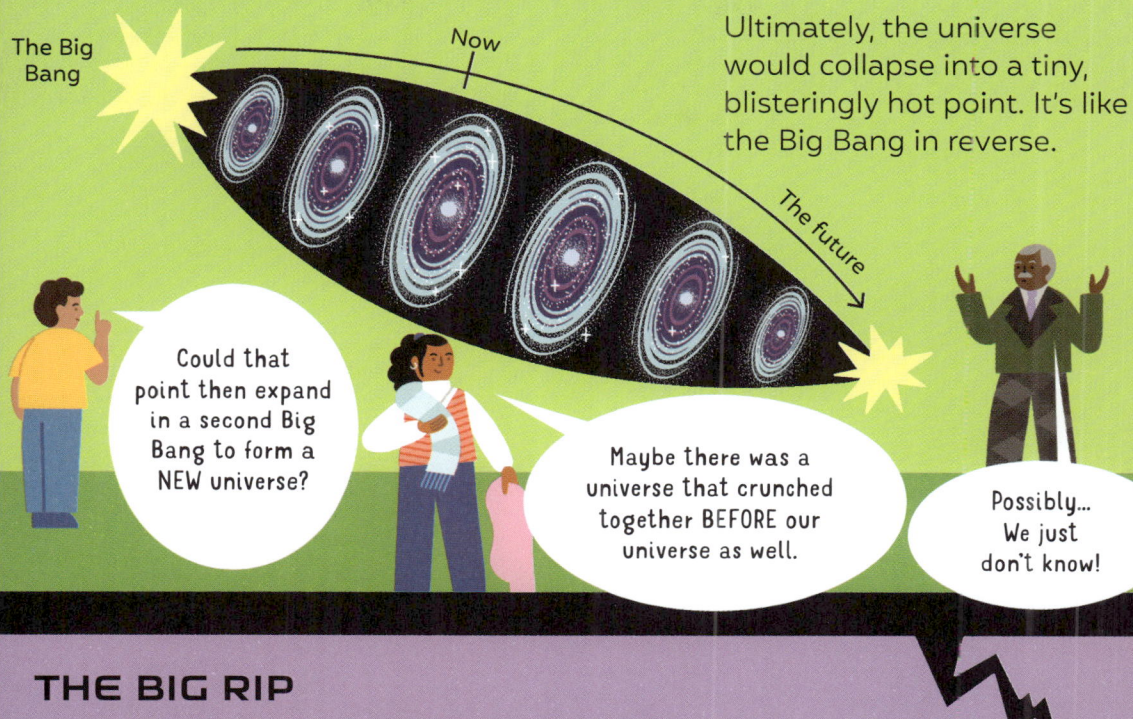

WHAT SHAPE IS THE UNIVERSE?

The key to how the universe works and how it will end could be its shape. Astronomers are trying to figure out what that is, but there are endless possibilities. Here are a few...

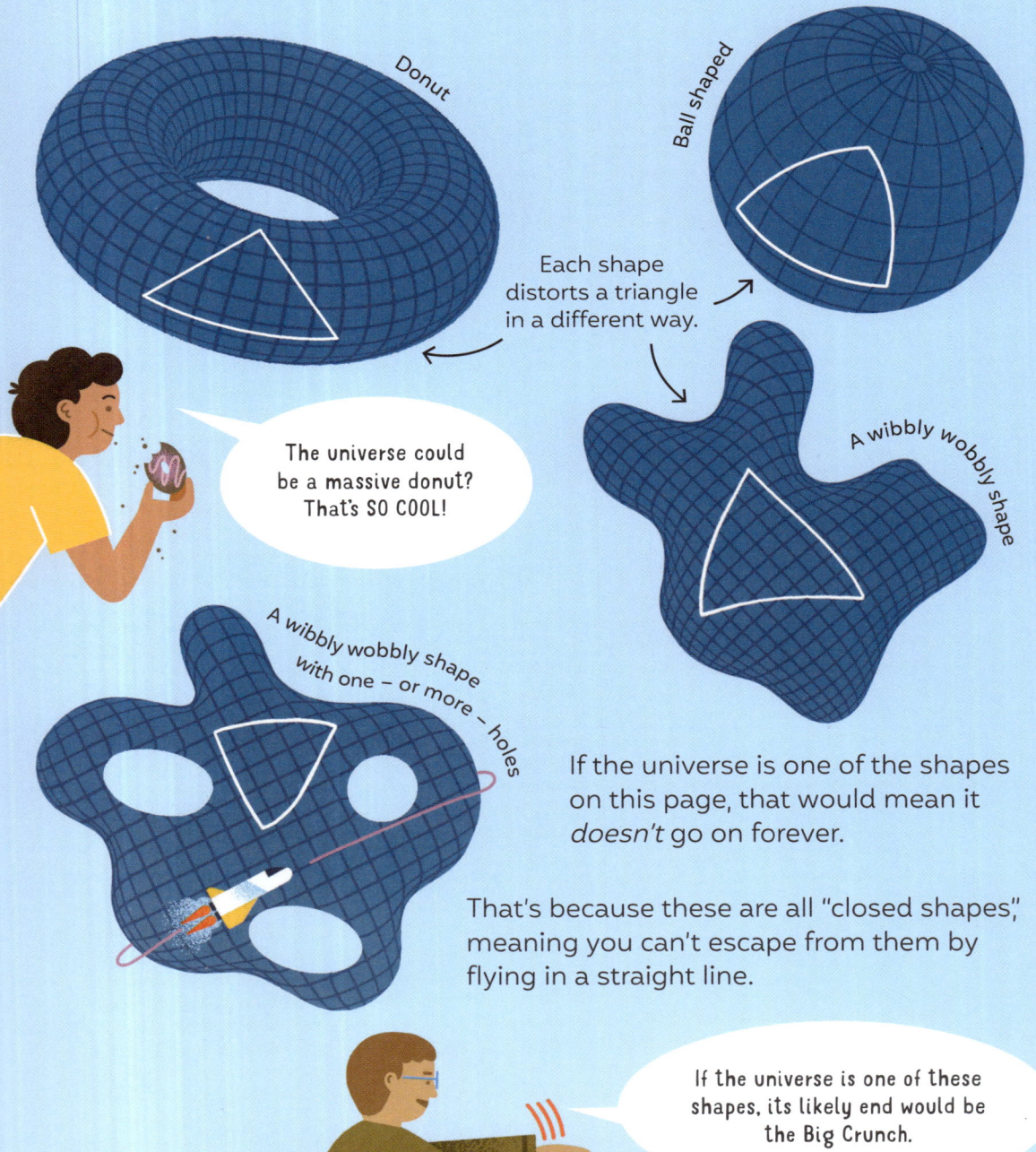

Donut

Ball shaped

Each shape distorts a triangle in a different way.

A wibbly wobbly shape

The universe could be a massive donut? That's SO COOL!

A wibbly wobbly shape with one – or more – holes

If the universe is one of the shapes on this page, that would mean it *doesn't* go on forever.

That's because these are all "closed shapes", meaning you can't escape from them by flying in a straight line.

If the universe is one of these shapes, its likely end would be the Big Crunch.

If the universe is one of the shapes on *this* page, that would mean it could stretch out FOREVER in all directions.

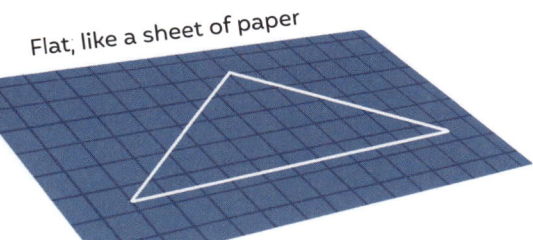

Flat, like a sheet of paper

A flat universe would end with the Big Freeze.

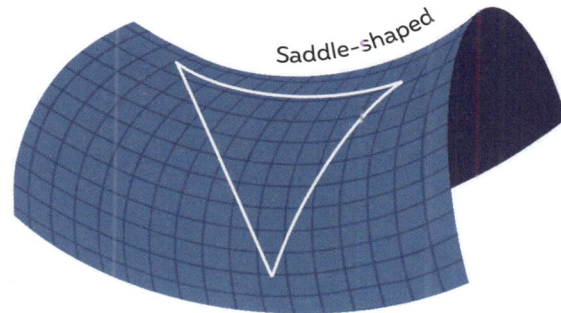

Saddle-shaped

Astronomers think a saddle-shaped universe would expand faster and faster, and end with the Big Rip.

Why do the triangles matter?

Look at their shapes. Do you see how they're all distorted except for the one on the flat universe?

Yeah... the triangle on the ball universe bulges out and the one on the saddle universe is squeezed.

Astronomers actually measure vast triangles in space to see whether or not they're distorted. It's how they hope to find out what shape the universe is.

And?

So far, the triangles don't appear at all distorted... Our universe seems to be as close to flat as we can measure.

But it's possible the universe is just WAY TOO VAST for us to detect any distortion.

What we're doing might be like trying to detect that *the Earth* is curved by measuring a triangle drawn on the floor.

MANY UNIVERSES?

There are lots of things we still don't know about the universe. But what if it's not even the *only one*?

One theory, known as **eternal inflation**, says that new universes are forming all the time – like bubbles in an orange soda.

They might be similar to ours... or they might follow COMPLETELY different rules.

Another theory, known as **many worlds**, says that when tiny particles, known as quantum particles, do *one thing* on Earth, in OUR universe...

...they also do *every other possible thing* in separate parallel universes.

Right now, there's no way to observe other universes, so we might never know if either of these theories is true. In fact, we can't even see all of OUR universe. So, you *could* think of everything we can't see as a separate universe.

The very idea that multiple universes exist might sound far-fetched, but so was the idea that other galaxies existed beyond the Milky Way – until it was proven...

GRAVITY

Gravity is what keeps our feet firmly on Earth. It's the pull that holds planets and stars together, and keeps everything in orbit. Put simply, gravity is the glue holding the universe together. Without it, everything would fall apart.

Gravity might just be the most important idea in astronomy. Astronomers are figuring out how gravity interacts with space and time, and how the incredibly strong gravity of black holes works. They've even detected gravitational waves from across the universe.

THE PULL OF GRAVITY

All the stuff, or **matter**, in the universe exerts a pull called gravity. We can only feel the pull of things that contain LOTS of matter, such as stars and planets. The more matter something has, the STRONGER its gravity.

Earth's gravity is what pulls us to the ground. We experience it every day in our own weight...

...and in the weight of objects around us. HEAAAAVE!

Here on Earth, people often confuse weight with something called mass (the amount of matter in something). But they're VERY different things.

MASS is how much matter something contains. Astronomers measure it in units called **KILOGRAMS (kg)**.

When you stand on a scale to "weigh" yourself, you're actually getting a figure for your mass.

VS.

WEIGHT is how hard gravity pulls on mass. It's measured in units called **NEWTONS (N)**.

On Earth, gravity pulls at a rate of 9.8 newtons for every kg of mass – or 9.8N/kg.

That's better!

Out in space, away from Earth's gravity, things still have mass, but they're almost weightless.

I'm so strong!

That's cheating, Nico!

Whooaaa... I can jump so high!

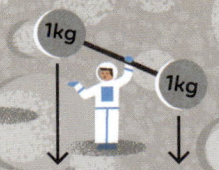

The Moon's gravity is about 6 times weaker than Earth's. It pulls at about 1.625N/kg.

Jupiter is MUCH more massive than Earth, so its gravity is stronger. It pulls at about 24.7N/kg. Even if the planet had a surface you could stand on, it'd be difficult to stand.

So... heavy...

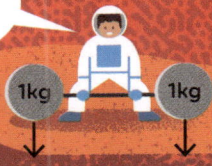

I can barely lift my legs!

Most of the time, it's enough to think of gravity like this – as a pull. But gravity has some bizarre effects on space and time. To make sense of those, astronomers have a different way of thinking about gravity. Turn the page to find out more.

SPACETIME

To understand how gravity *really* works, astronomers first have to think about how space and time work.

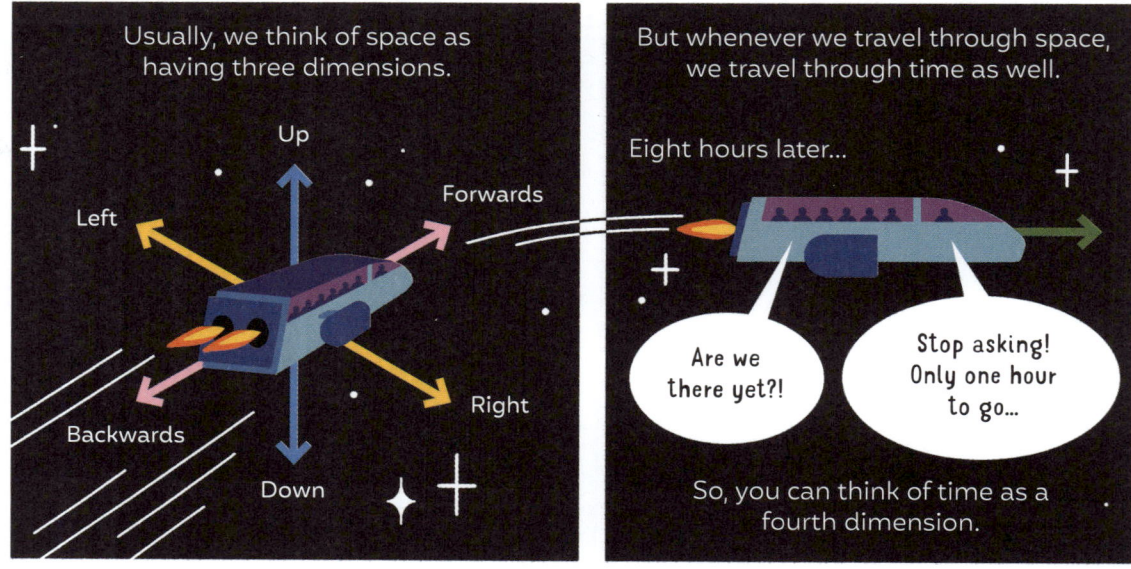

Astronomers imagine the three dimensions of space woven together with time, to make a single, four-dimensional thing called **spacetime**.

Now here's where it gets really interesting. Spacetime warps and bends when you add an object with lots of mass, such as a star.

This curving of spacetime explains the effects of gravity astronomers observe in the universe. For instance, orbiting...

TIMEWARP

When it comes to spacetime, space and time are impossible to separate. So, when a massive object warps the shape of space, it warps *time* too – with weird consequences...

Imagine you have two identical clocks, exactly in time with each other.

You send one clock into space, where there's very little gravity and spacetime is barely curved.

The other clock stays on Earth, where spacetime is warped due to Earth's mass.

The clock on Earth would actually tick a TINY bit slower than the one in space because time is stretched. So, it would show a different time.

Movement affects time as well. The FASTER you move, the SLOWER time passes for you.

Imagine your teacher zoomed off into space for a week at almost the speed of light – that's much faster than any real rocket can go.

When your teacher returned to Earth, one week would have passed for her, but several weeks would have passed on Earth.

So, what time it is depends on the shape of spacetime where you are, and how fast you're moving. It sounds far-fetched, but these timewarping effects have real-life consequences. Take location-mapping GPS satellites...

Sitting high above Earth's atmosphere, where gravity is weaker, the clocks on GPS satellites tick faster than clocks on Earth.

But these satellites also orbit at incredible speeds, which has the opposite effect, making their clocks tick more slowly.

Taken together, the lack of gravity has a slightly bigger impact. So, the clocks on GPS satellites gain about 0.000038 seconds a day.

This fraction of a second difference could cause the satellite to misjudge your location by 11km (7 miles)!

Eek... it says we're in the middle of that lake...

I think it's working now. Our locator dot has moved to a field.

The clocks on GPS satellites have to be adjusted many times a day to account for this.

BLACK HOLES

Despite the name, black holes aren't holes at all. Instead, they're the opposite: INCREDIBLY dense clusters of mass. And that means they exert mind-bogglingly strong gravity.

WHERE DO BLACK HOLES COME FROM?

There are several types of black hole.

Stellar mass black holes
The remains of dead stars. When the most massive stars explode, their cores collapse in on themselves. This crams lots of mass into a *very* small space.

Supermassive black holes
The biggest black holes. Astronomers aren't entirely sure where they come from. They may form when massive gas clouds collapse or when bigger black holes eat smaller ones.

Intermediate black holes
Middle-sized black holes. Astronomers think they form when smaller black holes join up.

The enormous amount of mass crammed into the middle of a black hole generates extraordinarily strong gravity – strong enough to rip apart planets and stars if they get too close.

The middle point is unimaginably dense. Scientists call it the **singularity**.

However a black hole forms, and whatever its size, they all seem to work in the same way…

I used to think that black holes were cosmic vacuum cleaners, sucking in everything around them. Actually, objects have to get PRETTY close before they fall inside. Stars can safely orbit black holes from a distance.

NO ESCAPE?

Dense clusters of mass with extreme-strength gravity might sound unusual. But, actually, astronomers think the universe could be teeming with them.

We think supermassive black holes exist in the middle of almost EVERY galaxy. And we can see hundreds of billions of galaxies...

GULP... So... That means there are hundreds of billions of supermassive black holes! Surely we can't avoid them forever?!

Don't panic, Nico! You'd have to get VERY close to a black hole to fall in. There are millions in the Milky Way – but the nearest one is more than 1,500 light-years away.

PHEW! But what would happen if I *did* fall into one?

Good question. Look what a black hole would do to our trampoline... umm... I mean SPACETIME.

Whoa! Does it go down forever? I can't see the bottom... ARGHHHH!

"Imagine Nico did fall into a black hole. Here's what would happen..."

The black hole's intense gravity would stretch Nico out like a piece of spaghetti. Astronomers call this process **spaghettification**.

Spacetime gets seriously warped by black holes. To Nico, time would pass normally. But to us, looking in from the outside, Nico would freeze in time as he approached the event horizon. It would look to us as though time had stopped for him.

Nico would be able to see out from inside the black hole. But if he crossed the event horizon, Nico would become invisible to us. That's because no light can escape beyond this point.

Event horizon

This is a silly example, but it raises some interesting questions that astronomers aren't able to answer yet.

Would Nico ever be able to escape the black hole? Or would he be lost in there forever?

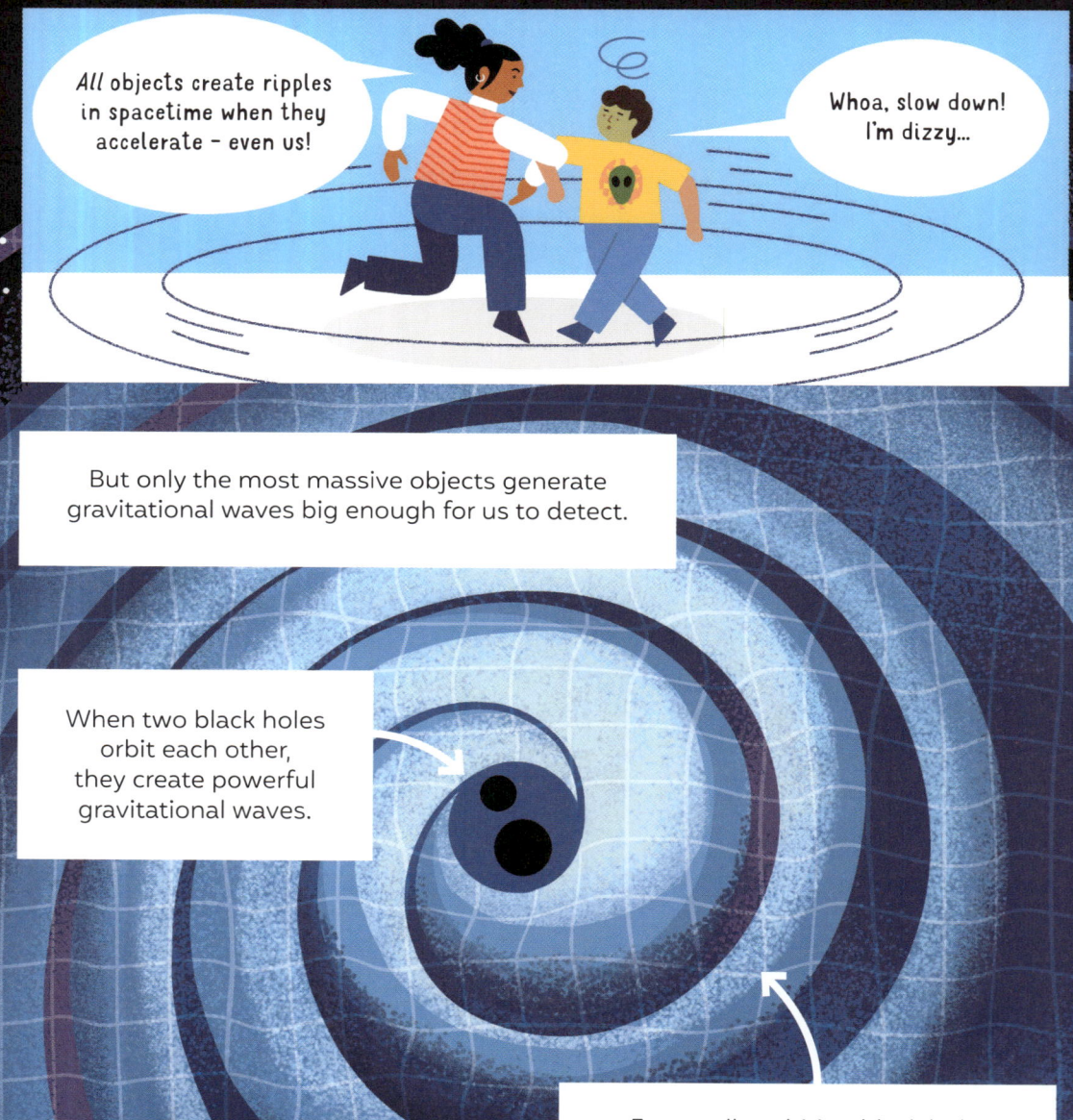

As those gravitational waves move through the universe, they warp the shape of spacetime around everything they pass. But they're tricky to detect.

Besides, even the most powerful gravitational waves are very weak once they reach Earth. So, astronomers use a super-sensitive observatory called LIGO to detect them. Here's how it works...

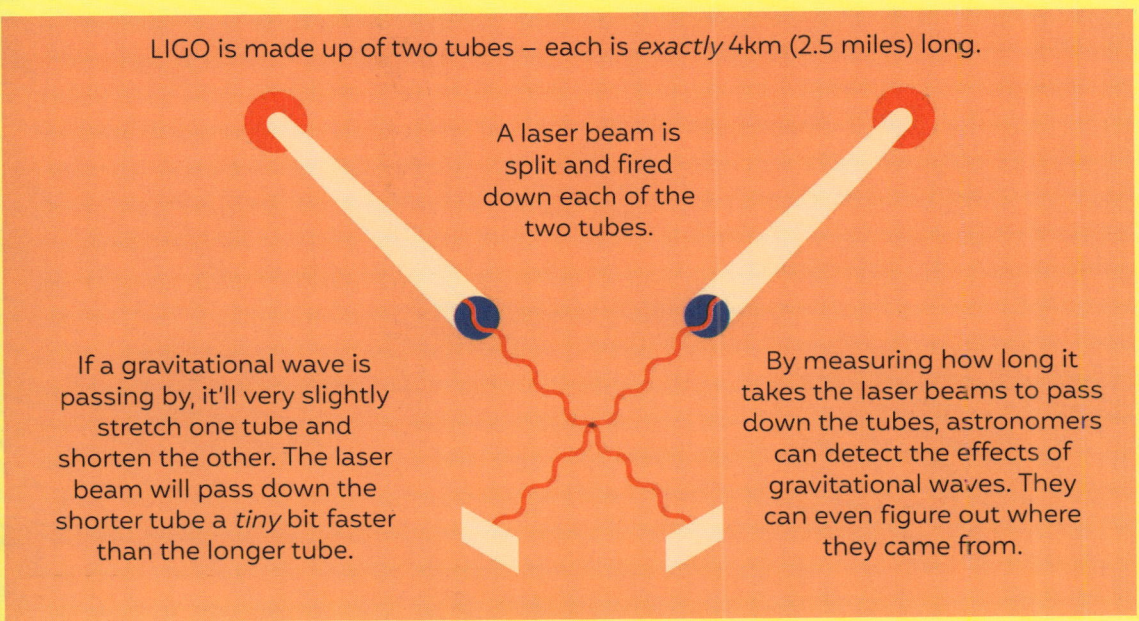

Scientists at LIGO first succesfully detected gravitational waves from two colliding black holes in 2015. So, now we have a whole new way of looking at the universe.

SPACETIME SHORTCUTS

One of the biggest obstacles to space travel is the sheer size of the universe. Imagine some aliens have invited you to a party...

"Lola, we've got to leave right now! We can't be late – the future of human-alien relations depends on it."

"Bad news, Nico. The party's tomorrow... and it's millions of light-years away."

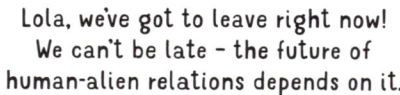

TO THE ALIEN PARTY

Theoretically, however, human-alien relations *could* be saved if Lola and Nico took a strange tunnel between points in spacetime called a **wormhole**. For this to work, the area of spacetime between the humans and the alien party would need to bend back on itself, like this.

TRAVEL TIME: 15 MILLION YEARS

TRAVEL TIME: 1 HOUR

If there was a wormhole between the humans and the party, it would cut out a HUGE distance.

ALIEN PARTY

"Hello, humans! How was your journey?"

"Hello, aliens! It went by in a flash – we took a wormhole."

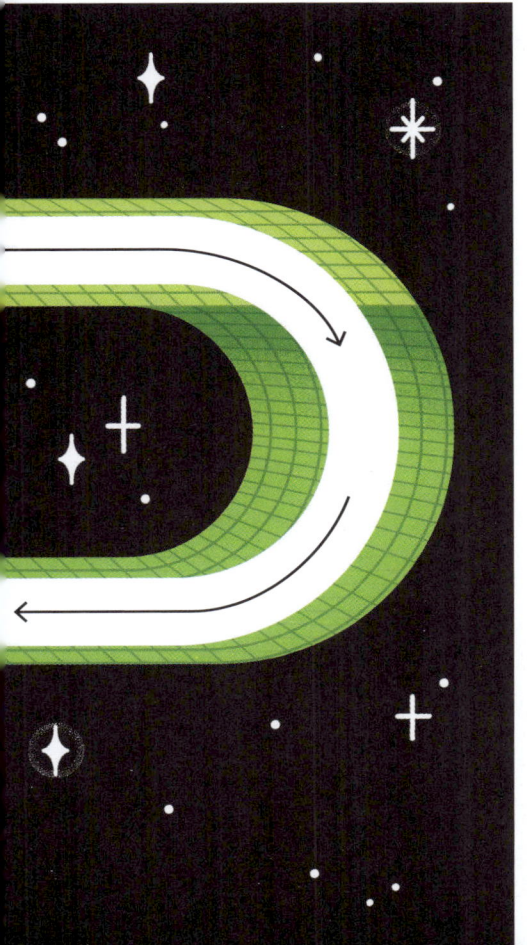

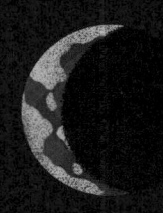

IS THERE ANYBODY OUT THERE?

Have you ever gazed up at the stars and wondered if there could be life out there, somewhere? Maybe an alien on a distant planet is wondering the same thing.

An entire branch of astronomy, called **astrobiology**, is dedicated to finding the answer. Astronomers have discovered lots of places in the universe that they think *could* support life. But we may never know for sure whether they do.

Who knows? It's also possible that humans will move out to other parts of the universe, becoming aliens themselves...

LOOKING FOR LIFE

When you're searching for something, it helps to know what you're looking for. That's why the search for life elsewhere in the universe starts with the study of life right here on Earth.

We think life started in Earth's oceans about 3.8 billion years ago. Water is the key. It turns out all life on Earth needs it.

So... the earliest animals were fish?

No! Fish first evolved around 300 million years ago. The earliest life forms were microbes – TINY specks you need a microscope to see. Our best guess is that they lived in deep underwater vents.

Surely there's no way to spot microbes on another planet with a telescope?!

Correct... We wouldn't even be able to see a large creature like a dinosaur on a distant planet. What we CAN search for is signs of water.

Signs of water can be detected by looking at what chemicals planets contain. And that's possible by studying the light telescopes collect from them – remember this from page 47?

HABITABLE WORLDS?

Astronomers think as many as a quarter of the planets out there could have water. With thousands of potential habitable worlds, where should the search for life begin?

OPERATION: FIND SOME ALIENS

"OK team, I've selected five possible planets. They're all kind of like Earth. Earth's the only place we know life exists, so it makes sense to start with one of these."

TRAPPIST-1E

- Orbits a dwarf star known as Trappist-1
- Similar size and density to Earth
- Might have an atmosphere similar to Earth's
- It's the right distance from the star for water to be liquid

"This is where we should look for aliens – it's perfect. Let's check it out!"

"Not so fast, Nico. Trappist-1E is 40 light-years away. There's no way we can visit to look for aliens."

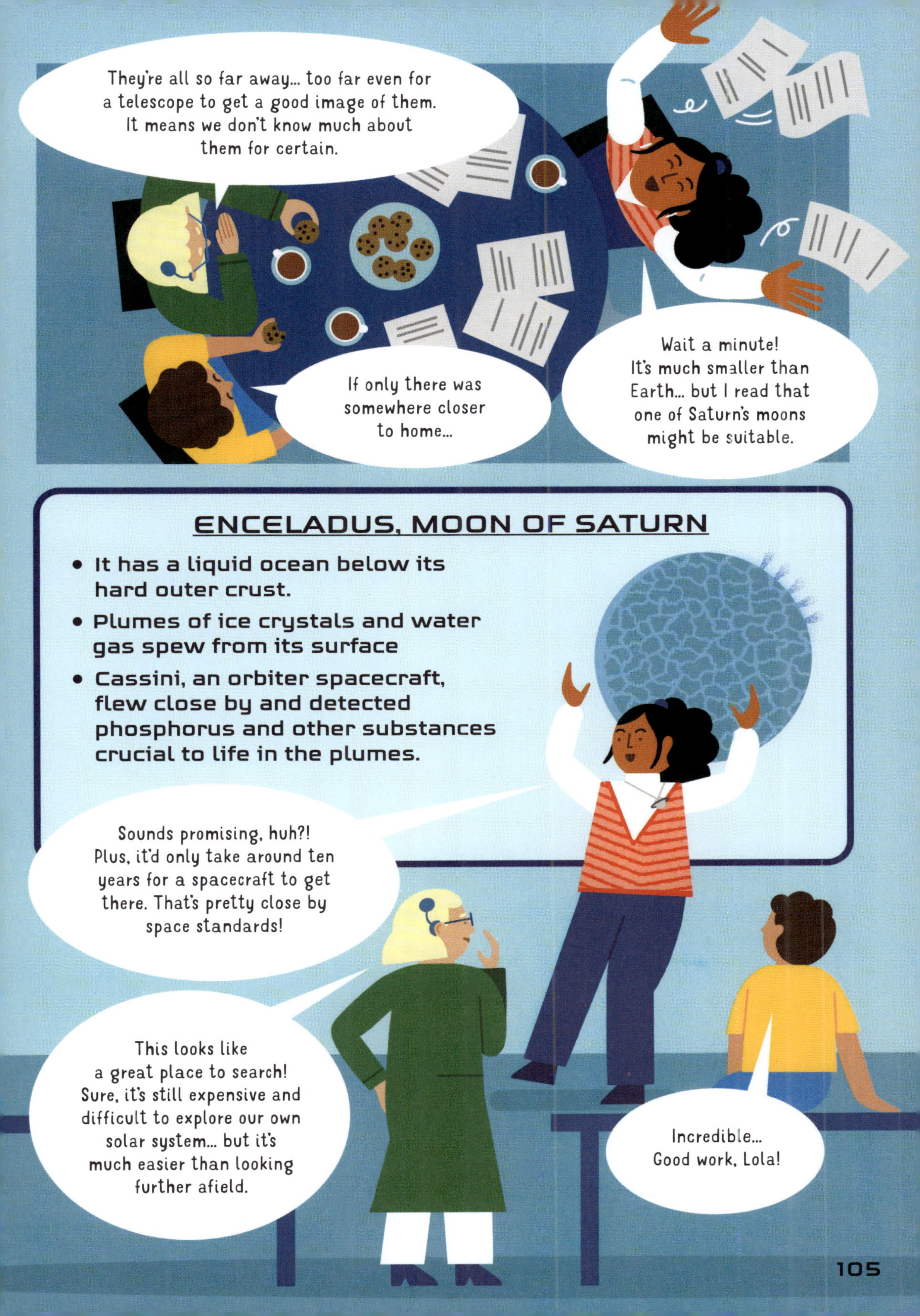

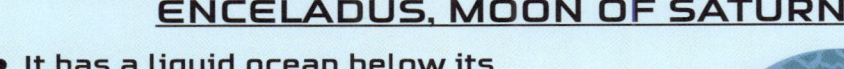

INTELLIGENT ALIENS?

Most places in the universe that might support life are *so* far away that we could never visit them to look for it. However, if one of them was home to INTELLIGENT life – with the technology to beam signals – we wouldn't need to visit to check.

Astronomers on Earth use an array of radio telescopes to scan the skies for signals that could be evidence of alien technology.

The telescopes are so sensitive they could pick up even a relatively weak signal – around the strength of an aircraft radar – from any of the nearest thousand stars!

And just in case there are aliens out there also wondering whether they're alone in the universe, astronomers have broadcast messages and songs into space.

...across the univerrrssse...

This song by the Beatles was the first one we broadcast. *Maybe* aliens out there were able to listen to it.

MOVING OUT

Life in space doesn't have to mean aliens. WE could be the ones to explore space further, maybe even setting up a colony on the Moon.

Moving out into space presents all kinds of challenges. But there's a space-based laboratory designed to investigate these challenges and develop solutions. It's called the International Space Station (ISS).

PROBLEM 1: Humans need WATER. But it's too heavy to take enough to last a long journey.

> 98% of water on the ISS is recycled. Water from astronauts' breath, sweat and urine is collected and filtered until it's clean.

> Astronauts drink recycled pee and sweat?! YUCK!

> It sounds disgusting, but the water we drink on Earth has been recycled several times as well.

PROBLEM 2: Getting OXYGEN to breathe.

The ISS can make its own by splitting water molecules into oxygen and hydrogen using electricity. But even with these clever methods, it still relies on deliveries of both water and oxygen from Earth.

PROBLEM 3: Growing FOOD to eat.

Astronauts on the ISS are doing experiments to figure out how to grow food in space.

> We grew this lettuce in space!

> It's so good to eat fresh food! Everything else we eat comes up from Earth – and definitely isn't fresh...

PROBLEM 4: The effects of SPACE on the HUMAN BODY

Away from Earth's gravity, astronauts' muscles and bones get weaker, because they don't have to work nearly as hard to hold them up.

The lack of gravity can affect their eyesight, too.

We have to exercise for two hours a day in space to keep our muscles working.

We astronauts take all kinds of measurements to see how our bodies are responding to conditions in space.

On top of that, high levels of radiation in space can increase astronauts' risk of cancer.

All the research carried out on the ISS and the technology developed for it could help scientists build a permanent settlement on the Moon. This would allow people to spend much longer periods of time there, and provide them with a base from which to explore further.

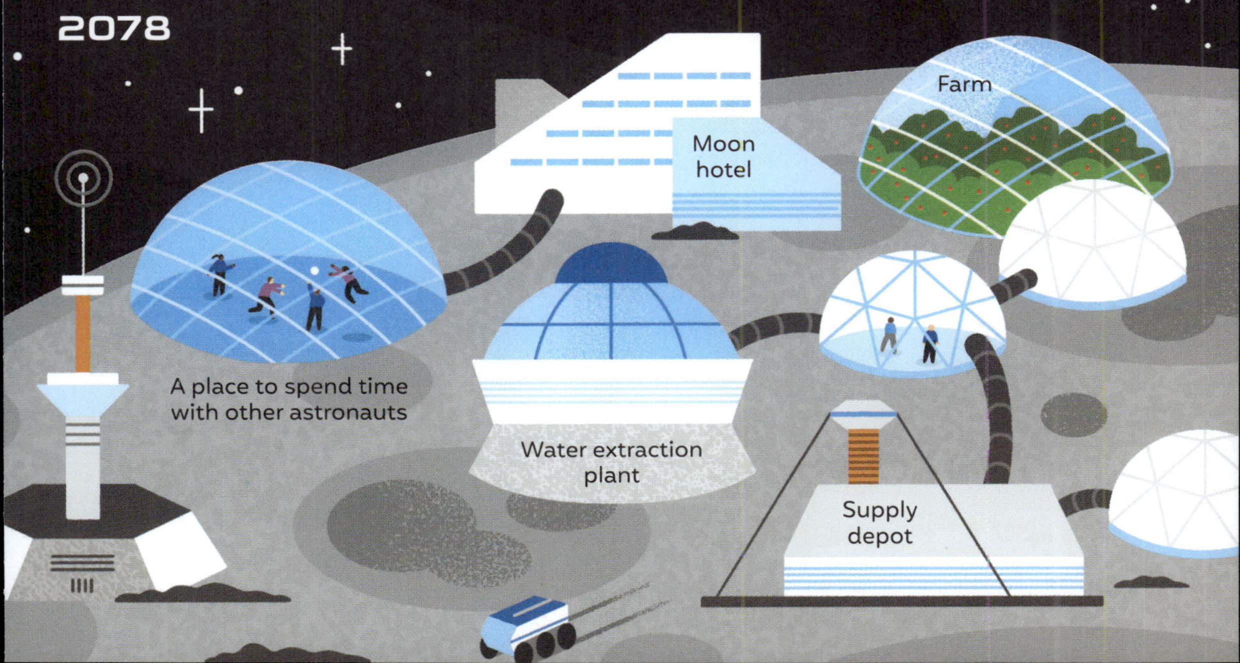

2078

A place to spend time with other astronauts

Moon hotel

Farm

Water extraction plant

Supply depot

WHO OWNS SPACE?

As space gets busier, and more and more countries venture out there, it's important to think about who – if anyone – it actually belongs to.

Since 1967, more than 100 countries have signed the **Outer Space Treaty**, a treaty managed by the United Nations, an international organization tasked with maintaining peace around the world.

OUTER SPACE TREATY

Space belongs to all humankind.

The Moon (and any other space objects) cannot be claimed by any nation.

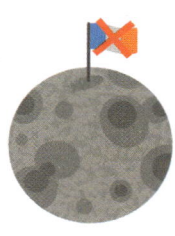

Space is to be used for peaceful purposes. Military bases and nuclear weapons are banned.

Astronauts are representatives of humankind.

Nations should share the results of their exploration of space with scientists around the world and the public.

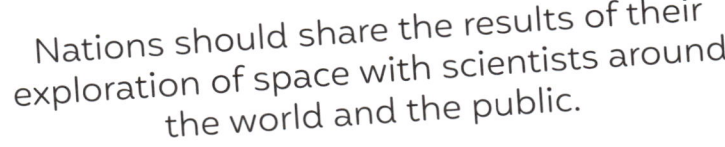

Nations should cooperate with, and assist, one another in the exploration of space.

ASTRONOMY AND YOU

Now that you know more about our amazing universe and how astronomers uncover its mysteries, perhaps you're wondering how YOU fit in. How does astronomy, with its big cosmic questions, affect your everyday life?

Read on to find out about some of the different jobs involved in understanding the universe, and about some of the puzzles astronomers are currently trying to solve. You'll also discover how ordinary people can take part in astronomy projects – and maybe even make discoveries of their own.

WANT TO FIND AN ALIEN?

You don't have to be a professional to make astronomical discoveries. Ordinary people can take part in projects, from spotting new comets to hunting for aliens, and become **citizen astronomers**. Some even find themselves in the news...

The Daily Stars
5,000th COMET DISCOVERED!

March 2024 – a student in the Czech Republic named Hanjie Tan has spotted a new comet. It's the 5,000th to be discovered using images from a sun-gazing satellite.

To make discoveries, citizen astronomers often scour through images or data from telescopes on their computers.

To find the comet, Hanjie Tan flicked through a sequence of images, until he spotted a speck of light moving in a straight line.

From 1999 to 2020, five million people helped look for aliens from the comfort of their homes.

THE WEEKLY POST
MASS ALIEN HUNT

March 2020 – five million people have downloaded a computer program that studies radio telescope data to pick up signs of extraterrestrial life. No aliens have been found... yet.

SHRRPPPPP

SHRRPPPPP

THE INTERNATIONAL GAZETTE

DUTCH TEACHER FINDS MYSTERY BLOB

June 2007 – Hanny van Arkel, a teacher from the Netherlands, has spotted a mystery bluey-green blob.

Hanny van Arkel was checking images of galaxies, when she saw a strange blob.

Professional astronomers couldn't work out what the blob was for ten years. Now they think it's a cloud of gas from a galaxy, lit up by a beam of light from a nearby black hole.

It was named "Hanny's Voorwerp," after me. That means "Hanny's object" in Dutch.

Oooo! That could be us! Should we get involved in a citizen astronomy project?

Yes! Can't wait!

Big telescope projects and space agencies, such as NASA, often have lists of astronomy projects that ordinary people can take part in from home.

For links to websites with citizen science projects, scan the code or visit **usborne.com/Quicklinks**

117

ASTRONOMY OF THE FUTURE

Since the first astronomers plotted the routes of stars across the skies, we've discovered millions of galaxies, found out how stars work and sent robots to Mars. What's next?

More accurate, powerful telescopes on Earth and in space will help astronomers look further into space, all the way back to the universe's first starlight.

Astronomers are studying the highest energy processes in the universe, such as black hole collisions and exploding supernovas.

ASTRONOMY JOBS

Do you want a career focused on our incredible universe? You could work from an observatory, in a university – or even in space!

OBSERVATIONAL ASTRONOMER

Observational astronomers collect and study data from space telescopes and observatories on Earth.

THEORETICAL ASTRONOMER

Theoretical astronomers come up with theories to *explain* the things that observational astronomers *see*. They make predictions about how stars, planets, moons, asteroids, comets, galaxies and black holes work, using computer simulations.

COSMOLOGIST

It's the job of a cosmologist to explore huge questions about the whole universe. They look into things such as the Big Bang, dark matter and dark energy. They work with enormous amounts of data, mathematical equations and computer models.

PLANETARIUM ASTRONOMER

Planetarium astronomers know all about astronomy and are also great at telling stories. They make hi-tech shows about the universe. These are projected onto the walls and ceiling of a large, dome-shaped room called a planetarium.

Woowwwwww!

ASTRONOMY TEACHER

It's the job of teachers to educate the next generation of astronomers. They help make sense of complex ideas about astronomy for university students. Many of them do their own research alongside teaching.

The life of a large star ends with an incredible explosion!

ASTRONAUT

If you want to work in space itself, you *could* become an astronaut. While they're up there, astronauts do all sorts of science experiments. They also support astronomers by taking photos of Earth, the Moon and eclipses, and by servicing space telescopes.

ASTROBIOLOGIST

Astrobiologists look for life beyond Earth. They try to identify any habitable environments and any possible signs of alien life. To help them know what to look for, they also research the origins of life on Earth.

121

GLOSSARY

This glossary explains some of the words used in this book. Words in *italics* are explained in other entries.

alien a lifeform from outer space

asteroid a small rocky object that orbits the Sun

astrobiology a branch of astronomy focused on finding out whether *aliens* exist

atmosphere a layer of gases surrounding some *planets* and *moons*

Big Bang the start of the *universe*, when all *matter* and energy rapidly expanded from a single, scorchingly hot point

black hole a very dense cluster of *mass*, which exerts such strong *gravity* that no *matter* or light can escape

brown dwarf a failed *star* that's bigger than a *planet*, but not big enough to be a star

citizen astronomy when ordinary people take part in astronomy research

comet a clump of ice and dust that has a long tail when it's near the Sun

cosmic microwave background, CMB leftover *radiation* from the *Big Bang*

dark energy a form of energy that we don't fully understand, which is causing the accelerating expansion of the *universe*

dark matter a mystery type of *matter* that's a source of *gravity*, but can't be easily detected

dwarf planet an object in space that's too small to count as a *planet*

Earth where we live – the third *planet* from the Sun in the *solar system*

eclipse when the light from one object, such as the Sun, gets blocked by something else passing in front of it, such as the Moon

electromagnetic spectrum *radiation*, such as light, X-rays and microwaves, that travels through space as *waves*

fusion when atoms combine releasing lots of energy. The Sun's heat and light are created through the fusion of hydrogen into helium

Goldilocks zone the region around a *star* where the temperature is "just right" for liquid water to exist on a *planet*

gravitational waves ripples in *spacetime* caused by the acceleration of large objects

gravity the pull exerted by all *matter*

Hubble Space Telescope a large space *telescope* currently in orbit around *Earth*

International Space Station (ISS) a large research lab orbiting *Earth*

Keck Observatory a place for observing space near the summit of Mauna Kea in Hawaii, with two enormous *telescopes*

light-year the distance light travels in a year (9,461,000,000,000 km or 5,880,000,000,000 miles), used to measure vast distances in space

LIGO a large scientific observatory structured around two long tubes, which are used to detect *gravitational waves*

mass the amount of *matter* something contains, measured in kilograms

mathematical model a way of thinking about how things in the *universe* behave, using equations

matter all the "stuff" in the *universe*

meteorite strike when a *meteoroid* passes through *Earth's* atmosphere and hits Earth

meteoroid a small space rock, which is a fragment of an *asteroid* or *comet*

Milky Way the name of our galaxy, a vast spiral of *stars*

moon a natural *satellite* which orbits a *planet*

multiverse an idea that there are multiple *universes*, existing at the same time

neutron star the collapsed core of a huge *star*, left behind after a *supernova*

observational astronomy a branch of astronomy which involves collecting and analyzing data from telescopes on *Earth* or in space

orbit the curved path taken by one object around another, for instance by a *planet* around a *star*, or a *moon* around a planet

Outer Space Treaty an agreement between countries about how to behave in space

planet an object in orbit around a *star*, large enough to have cleared other objects out of its way

probe a spacecraft without a crew, designed to send information about space down to *Earth*

radiation energy transmitted through space as *waves*. Some types can be harmful to humans in large quantities.

redshift when the wavelength of light gets stretched, making it look redder

rover a type of *probe* designed to travel across the surface of a *planet* or *moon*

satellite an object which orbits a *planet*

singularity an unimaginably dense point used to describe the earliest conditions in the *universe* and those in the middle of a *black hole*

solar system the region of space in which *planets*, *moons* and *asteroids* are held in orbit around the Sun

space the cold emptiness beyond *Earth's atmosphere* and between *stars*, *planets* and other space objects

space junk debris left over from space missions and broken satellites, which orbits *Earth*

spacetime the fabric of the *universe*, which combines time and the three dimensions of space

spectroscopy examining light from a *star* to find out which chemicals the star contains

star a huge ball of hot, glowing gas that makes its own heat and light

supernova an enormous explosion at the end of a *star's* life

telescope an instrument that allows you to see distant objects more clearly

theoretical astronomy a branch of astronomy that uses models to predict and explain how the *universe* works

universe everything that exists – all *matter*, time, space and energy

visible light the part of the *electromagnetic spectrum* that we can see

waves ripples which carry energy from one point to another

white dwarf the hot, dense leftover core of a *star* that has come to the end of its life

wormhole tunnels between different points in *spacetime* that could allow you to travel huge distances very quickly – if they actually exist

INDEX

Aldrin, Buzz, 27

alien, 5, 98-99, 100-111, 116, 119, 121, 122

Andromeda, 33, 55

Armstrong, Neil, 27

asteroid, 4, 14, 24-25, 40, 60, 120, 122

astrobiology, 100-103, 121, 122

atmosphere, 4, 19, 21, 22, 25, 34, 38-39, 40, 52-53, 91, 103, 104, 122

Betelgeuse, 46

Big Bang, 68-73, 78-79, 120, 122

Big Crunch, 79, 80

Big Freeze, 78, 81

Big Rip, 79, 81

black hole, 5, 85, 92-97, 115, 117, 118, 120, 122

brown dwarf, 58, 62, 122

Chandra X-ray Observatory, 51

citizen astronomy, 116-117, 122

comet, 4, 24, 40, 116, 120, 122

Copernicus, Nicolaus, 11

coronal mass ejections, 19

cosmic microwave background, CMB, 73, 122

dark energy, 77, 79, 118-119, 120, 122

dark matter, 5, 74-75, 77, 79, 118-119, 120, 122

dwarf planets, 24, 37, 122

Earth, 4, 6-8, 10-23 25-29, 30-35, 38-41, 49, 50, 53, 54-55, 69, 81, 83, 85-87, 90-91, 97, 102-109, 111, 114, 118, 120-121, 122

eclipse, 8-9, 121, 122

Eddington, Arthur, 60

Einstein, Albert, 61

electromagnetic spectrum, 49, 52-53, 122

Enceladus, 105

eternal inflation theory, the 83

frequency, 45, 49

fusion, 58, 61, 122

Gagarin, Yuri, 26

Galileo Galilei, 11, 32

gamma rays, 49

GN-z11, 55

Goldilocks zone, 20, 122

gravity, 18, 21, 22-23, 58-59, 60, 64, 67, 74-77, 79, 84-95, 109, 123

Hubble, Edwin, 33

Hubble Space Telescope, 39, 62, 76, 123

Huygens, Christiaan, 32
Huygens (space probe), 40

infrared, 48-49, 53, 114
International Space Station (ISS), 27, 29, 103, 108-109, 111, 123

Jupiter, 14-17, 24, 40, 65, 87

Keck Observatory, 37, 123
Kuiper Belt, 15, 37

LIGO, 97, 118, 123
Lucretius, 63

magnetosphere, 21
many-worlds theory, 83
Mars, 12, 14, 16, 20, 24, 41, 118
mass, 61, 86-87, 89, 90, 92, 94, 123
mathematical model, 57, 64-65, 74, 77, 120, 123
Mercury, 14-16
meteoroid, 4, 24-25, 123
meteorite strike, 25, 123
microwaves, 49, 72, 122
Milky Way, 11, 18, 33, 39, 46, 55, 56, 69, 76, 83, 94, 114, 123
Moon, the, 6-9, 14, 22-23, 24, 27, 87, 108-109, 110-111, 114, 121, 122

moon, 15, 25, 31, 40-41, 105, 107, 120, 123
multiverse, 82-83, 123

Neptune, 15, 16-17, 36
neutron star, 59, 123
New Horizons (space probe), 40
Newton, Isaac, 33
NGC 2775, 55

observatory, 34-37, 51, 97, 120, 123
Orion Nebula, 56
Outer Space Treaty, 110-111, 123

Payne-Gaposchkin, Cecilia, 61
Perseverance, 41
Planck space telescope, 73
planet, 4, 9, 10-11, 12-18, 20-25, 31-32, 35-37, 40-41, 52-53, 58, 65, 69, 78, 85-87, 89, 92, 101-104, 107, 118-119, 120, 123
probe, 27, 31, 40-41, 118, 123
    lander probe, 40
    flyby probe, 40
    rover, 41, 124
Proxima Centauri, 54-55
Ptolemy, 10

radiation, 21, 43, 49, 51, 52, 63, 72, 75, 103, 109, 114, 124

radio waves, 49, 53
redshift, 70-71, 124
Rigel, 46
rover, 41, 124

Saturn, 14-17, 32, 40, 105
singularity, the, 68, 92, 124
solar flares, 19
solar wind, 19
space junk, 28-29, 124
spacetime, 88-91, 94-99, 118, 124
spectrometer, 47
spectroscopy, 47, 115, 124
star, 4, 6-11, 14, 18-19, 25, 31, 33, 35, 37, 38-39, 43, 44, 46-47, 49, 54, 56, 58-65, 69, 70, 75, 76, 78, 85-86, 89, 92-93, 101, 104, 106, 112, 115, 118, 120-121, 124
Sun, the, 6, 8, 11, 13-22, 24, 27, 44, 46-47, 52, 54-55, 59, 60-61, 63, 65
supernova, 59, 118, 120, 124

telescope, 11, 15, 30-39, 40, 43, 47, 50-51, 57, 62, 72-73, 75, 76, 102, 105, 106, 116-117, 118, 120-121, 124

theoretical astronomy, 56-65, 120, 124
thought experiment, 63, 64
Trappist-1E, 104

ultraviolet, 49, 52
universe, 5, 9-11, 13, 31, 33, 39, 43, 49, 54, 57, 58-59, 63, 64, 66-83, 85, 86-87, 89, 94, 96-97, 98, 101, 102, 106, 113, 114, 118-119, 120-121, 124
Uranus, 15-17, 55

Venus, 14, 16, 52-53
visible light, 42-49, 52, 124
Von Helmholtz, Hermann, 60
Voyager 1 and 2, 27

wavelength, 45-47, 49, 52, 71-72
waves, 44-45, 48-49, 53, 71, 124
    gravitational, 85, 96-97, 123
weight, 86-87
white dwarf, 59, 124
wormhole, 98-99, 124

X-rays, 49, 51, 72

Photo credits:

pp.12-13 © Babak Tafreshi/Science Photo Library; pp30-31, 39 top © NASA, ESA, and S. Beckwith (STScI) and the HUDF Team; p39 bottom © NASA, ESA/Hubble and the Hubble Heritage Team, pp42-43, 51 © NASA/CXC/MIT/F.K. Baganoff et al.; p.50 top © NASA/CXC/MIT/F.K. Baganoff et al.; p.50 bottom © NASA/CXC/MIT/F.K. Baganoff et al.; p.52 top © NASA/Johns Hopkins University Applied Physics Laboratory/Carnegie Institution of Washington; p.52 bottom © ISAS/JAXA; p.53 top © ISAS/JAXA; p.53 bottom © NASA/JPL/USGS; pp.56-57 © NASA, G. Bacon, L. Frattare, Z. Levay, and F. Summers (STScI/AURA); p.73 © ESA and the Planck Collaboration; p.114 IRAS Imagery/ARC/NASA

First published in 2026 by Usborne Publishing Limited, 83-85 Saffron Hill, London EC1N 8RT, United Kingdom. usborne.com

Copyright © 2026 Usborne Publishing Limited. The name Usborne and the Balloon logo are registered trade marks of Usborne Publishing Limited. All rights reserved. No part of this publication may be reproduced or used in any manner for the purpose of training artificial intelligence technologies or systems (including for text or data mining), stored in retrieval systems or transmitted in any form or by any means without prior permission of the publisher. UE.